GARY R. COLLINS

Can You Trust

PSYCHOLOGY?

Exposing the Facts & the Fictions

INTERVARSITY PRESS
DOWNERS GROVE, ILLINOIS 60515

©1988 by Gary R. Collins

InterVarsity Press is the book-publishing division of InterVarsity Christian Fellowship, a student movement active on campus at hundreds of universities, colleges and schools of nursing. For information about local and regional activities, write Public Relations Dept., InterVarsity Christian Fellowship, 6400 Schroeder Rd., P.O. Box 7895, Madison, WI 53707-7895.

Distributed in Canada through InterVarsity Press, 860 Denison St., Unit 3, Markham, Ontario L3R 4H1, Canada.

All Scripture quotations, unless otherwise indicated, are from the Holy Bible, New International Version. Copyright © 1973, 1978, International Bible Society. Used by permission of Zondervan Bible Publishers.

Cover illustration: Roberta Polfus

ISBN 0-8308-1710-7 (paper)
ISBN 0-8308-1725-5 (cloth)

Printed in the United States of America

Library of Congress Cataloging in Publication Data

Collins, Gary R.
    Can you trust psychology?: exposing the facts & the fictions/
Gary Collins.
        p.   cm.
    Bibliography: p.
    Includes index.
    ISBN 0-8308-1710-7
    1. Psychology and religion.   2. Christianity—Psychology.
3. Psychology—Philosophy.   4. Counseling—Philosophy.   I. Title.
BF51.C64 1988
150—dc19   87-37384
                                                            CIP

---

17   16   15   14   13   12   11   10   9   8   7   6   5   4   3   2   1
99   98   97   96   95   94   93   92   91   90   89   88

To My Respected Colleagues
at Trinity

David E. Carlson, ACSW
David E. Dillon, EdD
Jan P. Hook, MA
G. Al Masterson, MD
David J. McKay, PhD
Michael J. Pearson, ACSW
William L. Secor, PhD

With deep appreciation for
their Christian commitment,
professional competence,
continuing friendship
and intellectual stimulation

Preface

I wonder what ever happened to old-fashioned college debating societies.

Probably they still exist, as they have for centuries, in the esteemed colleges of Cambridge and Oxford. But could any of those fine British institutions begin to match the grand debating duels that took place in my little alma mater?

Most exciting were the periodic faculty debates. Sometimes dressed in their resplendent academic robes, the professorial debaters would process into the debating room, solemnly marching behind the referee, who, for this auspicious occasion, was given the title of moderator.

The debate topics were always designed to delight undergraduate audiences.

Resolved: The most useless people in the world are professors!

Resolved: People who can't think become philosophers!

Resolved: People in their right minds never run for President!

In mock seriousness, the debaters would present their persuasive speeches with vigor, humor, impeccable English, marvelous metaphors, sweeping gestures and periodic punches at their opponents' ideas. When it was all over, members of the audience would vote for the winners, and everyone would go to the student union for refreshments. All of this was done good-naturedly. Even when the debaters tackled more serious topics, they tried to understand each other, and they avoided personal insult or character assassination.

I wish we could have more debaters like that today: people who believe strongly in their positions but who show respect for those who think differently. I wish we could learn to listen to one another and be sure our facts are correct before launching broadside attacks against people with whom we disagree.

Albert Ellis is a well-known and influential psychologist whose approach to counseling has been acclaimed by a variety of people-helpers, including some Christians. Ellis is a persuasive speaker and a powerful debater.

But he has no respect for religion or religious people. "Religion," he once wrote, "means at its core, some kind of faith unfounded on fact."[1] In his opinion, religion sabotages mental health, and religious people are masochistic, emotionally disturbed, stubborn, neurotic, obsessive-compulsive, motivated by anxiety, guilt-ridden, self-condemning, inflexible and unwilling to accept uncertainty in life. Ellis writes that religious people lack tolerance, but he seems to have no awareness of his own rigidity and intolerance.

Ellis holds an extreme position. Few psychologists share his strongly negative opinions about religion. But biased arguments such as these have helped make Christians fearful and suspicious of psychology.

When I was a freshman attending those faculty debates, there were people in our church who distrusted psychology. Many have changed their opinions over the years (especially as more and more courses in psychology and Christian counseling have been offered in Bible colleges and seminaries). But other believers have become increasingly opposed to the social sciences. Some sincere followers of Christ have wondered if psychology is a harmful, subtle scheme of the devil himself, the basis of a new religion for America.

Paul Vitz is a Christian who teaches psychology at New York University. In a widely acclaimed book, Vitz argues that psychology has become a religion, "a form of secular humanism based on worship of the self."[2] As a religion, says Vitz, psychology is strong, anti-Christian, and involved in destroying individuals, families and communities.

Other writers would agree. In his popular book *The Psychological Society*, Martin Gross maintains that traditional religion has weakened in Western society.[3] As a result, people are confused and inclined to consult "psychological experts" who replace theological truths with new scientific words and therapies.

These new scientific ideas, however, may be less powerful and effective than some of the experts claim. The twin sisters of psychology and psychiatry have been attacked by both secular and Christian writers. "The field is completely chaotic and divided," wrote Carl Rogers, the founder of client-centered therapy.[4] Psychiatry is in trouble, according to Christian counselor Jay Adams.[5] Psychiatric theory and practice are characterized by "personal helplessness, hopelessness and irresponsibility."[6]

Other writers argue that psychotherapy is a "theoretical sand castle" characterized by "much subjectivity, sentimentality, superstition, and even shamanism."[7] Within the psychological community today, says William Kirk Kilpatrick, there is "an abundance of speculation, wishful thinking, contradictory ideas, prejudice, doubletalk, and ideology disguised as science."[8] Psychology has good intentions, Kilpatrick suggests, but it is a seductive and dangerous wolf in sheep's clothing.[9] Evangelist Jimmy Swaggart was even more vehement when he told a television audience that psychology is "the rot of hell."

"Christian psychology" fares no better. It has been called "the most dangerous and at the same time the most appealing and powerful form of modernism ever to have invaded the church."[10] Another writer suggests that "Christian psychologist" is the same as "Christian witch doctor"—a contradiction in terms, an attempt to mix light with darkness in direct contradiction to 2 Corinthians 6:15.[11]

___ 11 ___

These are strong charges, made by deeply concerned and widely respected people.

Are their criticisms valid?

Is psychology the seductive, inaccurate and destructive force that its critics claim?

Could these critics be equally seductive, inaccurate and harmful?

Have some respected religious leaders been seduced into applauding and endorsing books that are sensationalist and persuasive but not completely accurate?

These questions are far more important and serious than the issues debated by my professors in mock solemnity many years ago.

Debates about the dangers and trustworthiness of psychology can be confusing to students, lay people, pastors, professional counselors and individuals who might need counseling help. Popular criticisms of psychology, many written by Christians, have been read widely and quoted often in college classrooms, counselors' offices and sermons. But nobody, to my knowledge, has attempted to write a balanced answer to psychology's critics.

Such is the purpose of this book. It is a challenge that I have not taken lightly or enthusiastically.

I know and respect many of the people who have criticized psychology. Many are fellow Christians; some are personal friends. I agree with some of their published criticisms and have no desire to defend those aspects of psychology that *are* weak.

In addition, I have no desire to be abrasive. I dislike argument and have no interest in producing a book that could be seen as an angry defense of psychology or a hostile counterattack on those who have been critical of my field. Instead, I have tried to write as a Christian gentleman who fully acknowledges valid criticisms, who has tried to graciously present a more balanced perspective on psychology, but who is willing to firmly challenge critics when they make statements that appear sensationalist, half-true or totally inaccurate.

Never before have I felt so strongly that a book forming in my mind needed to be put on paper. Never before have I so strongly resisted the tug to write. Never before have so many people urged me to continue with a writing project. They know who they are, and I am deeply grateful for their prayers and words of encouragement. Neil Ellison, Mark Mittelberg and my wife, Julie, have been especially helpful.

I realize that some readers will disagree with my interpretations and answers. I have tried, however, to produce a book that is Christ-honoring, fair, balanced, accurate and biblical. If the following pages clear up some of the confusion about psychology and help some readers, then my efforts will have been worthwhile.

Gary R. Collins
Kildeer, Illinois

PART 1
Questions about Getting Counseling

Can You Trust Psychology?

1

*B*ERNIE ZILBERGELD DOESN'T TRUST PSYCHOLOGY. DESPITE HIS PH.D. FROM Berkeley, his twelve years' experience as a practicing therapist, and his acclaim as a psychological researcher and author, Dr. Zilbergeld has written a whole book to criticize his own profession. Many psychological conclusions are really myths, he writes. Professional therapy is "overpromoted, overused, and overvalued."[1]

These criticisms could be dismissed had they come from a journalist or theologian writing as an outsider. But they come instead from a member of the psychological guild who has gone through all the prescribed training in clinical psychology, has been in therapy himself, has taken the time to interview 140 former patients, and has met for lengthy discussions with a cross-range of fourteen professional colleagues.

So impressive are Zilbergeld's writings that a prestigious Christian journal printed an excerpt from his book and asked some Christian counselors to give their reactions.[2] Each agreed that Zilbergeld's book included a lot of truth. One pastoral counselor responded that the weaknesses of psychology and psychiatry are so great (and so well documented by Zilbergeld's work) that Christians must stop "crawling around the psychiatrists' table looking for crumbs with which to 'supplement' what the Bible says."[3]

If psychology, psychiatry, psychotherapy and related fields are the objects of so much controversy, can they really be trusted? In the book of Romans, Paul urged believers "to watch out for those who cause divisions and put obstacles in your way that are contrary to the teaching you have learned. Keep away from them. For such people are not serving our Lord Christ, but their own appetites. By smooth talk and flattery they deceive the minds of naive people. Everyone has heard about your obedience, so I am full of joy over you; but I want you to be wise about what is good, and innocent about what is evil" (Rom. 16:17-19).

Is it possible that psychologists, including Christian psychologists, are among those who "deceive the minds of naive people," by smooth talk and unproven psychological myths? By listening to the teachings of psychology has the church "embraced an alien gospel administered by a new class of (psychological) priests supported by humanistic authority?"[4] Is it ever possible to trust psychology?

Many years ago I decided to study for a year at a theological seminary. The courses were interesting and helpful, especially because classes were small and students were able to interact freely with the godly, knowledgeable professors.

One day we got into a discussion about whether or not theology could be trusted. "It all depends on the theology and the theologian," our professor stated. Theology seeks to get accurate facts about God and how he relates to the universe—including human beings.[5] Unlike the Bible, which is the completely accurate and fully inspired Word of God, theology is subject to error because it depends on human understanding.

When the theologian seeks to be guided by the Holy Spirit and when the theology is based on a careful study of Scripture, then theology most likely can be trusted. When theology comes from individuals who give little heed to the Scriptures and who base their conclusions mostly on personal study and opinion, then theology is less likely to be trustworthy, regardless of the sincerity, scholarship and good intentions of the theologians.

Similar conclusions could be made about psychology. Can it be trusted? It all depends on the psychology and the psychologist.

When a psychologist seeks to be guided by the Holy Spirit, is committed to serving Christ faithfully, is growing in his or her knowledge of the Scriptures, is well aware of the facts and conclusions of psychology, and is willing to evaluate psychological ideas in the light of biblical teaching—then you can trust the psychologist, even though he or she at times will make mistakes, as we all do. If the psychology or psychological technique is not at odds with scriptural teaching, then it is likely to be trustworthy, especially if it also is supported by scientific data. But the Bible is the only writing that is infallible. Psychological conclusions, like theological statements, must be evaluated carefully before we accept or reject them.

When I was growing up in Canada, a local jeweler used to advertise on the radio, trying to attract business from couples who were thinking about engagement rings. The message was always the same: "If you don't know your diamonds, know your diamond man."

The same could be said about psychology: If you don't know your psychology, find a committed believer who can help you decipher what is valid and what may be counterfeit. Don't throw out everything simply because some psychology is weak and in error, any more than a jeweler would throw out his whole stock of rings because he found some glass stones among the gems.

When Jesus sent the disciples into the world he did not tell them to ignore the world's philosophies, but rather to be on guard. "I am sending you out like sheep among wolves," Jesus warned. "Therefore be as shrewd as snakes and as innocent as doves" (Mt 10:16). This is a good warning to keep in mind as we turn to more specific questions about the influence and teachings of modern psychology.

What do we mean by "psychology"? In college courses, most students learn that psychology is a science and academic field of study that seeks to understand and sometimes to change behavior. Psychology includes the study of mental disorders, and it deals with counseling and psychotherapy. But psychology involves much more. Some psychologists are sophisticated researchers. Others are skilled business or educational consultants. Many are experts in physiology, learning, perception, emotion, social issues, sleep disorders, human development, animal behavior, criminal justice, marketing, media influences, pastoral counseling, and a host of other specialties.

In the pages that follow, we will try to keep this broad meaning of *psychology* in mind. Many people use the word in a more popular way, however. They equate psychology with counseling, psychotherapy, psychiatry and psychological treatment. For the sake of simplicity and ease of discussion, we may also use some of these words interchangeably, even though they have different technical meanings. Psychology includes, but is not limited to, discussions about human problems and counseling.

Some psychological conclusions cannot be trusted and must not be accepted. But a lot of psychology *is* both trustworthy and helpful. The questions that follow cannot be dismissed or ignored by Christians who live in a psychological society. They are important questions that need clear answers.

Why Should a Christian Get Counseling If God Can Meet All Our Needs?

2

STUDENTS HAVE A WAY OF ASKING DIFFICULT QUESTIONS THAT KEEP THEIR teachers alert.

Consider, for example, this question from a seminary student who was wondering about the need for counseling. "Paul didn't sit around with the Corinthians building rapport and showing empathy," my student began. "The apostle boldly confronted the Corinthians with their sin, quoted Scripture, and told them to shape up. Why do we need counseling when Paul, who is a good role model, did nothing of the sort?"

I answered that Paul was indeed confrontational, but sometimes he could be very gentle. He debated with the people at Athens (Acts 17:16-43), discussed Scripture with the noble Bereans (Acts 17:11), hugged and cried with the Ephesians at Miletus (Acts 20:37), and instructed the

Galatians to bear each other's burdens and to restore people gently (Gal 6:1-2). It is not correct to suggest that he only advocated confrontation. He urged the Thessalonians to "warn those who are idle," but also to "encourage the timid, help the weak," and "be patient with everyone" (1 Thess 5:14). He gave guidance, encouragement, teaching and gentle advice—often in the form of sensitive and caring letters.

But now that we have Paul's letters and the rest of Scripture, why would anyone need counseling? This question was asked not by a student, but by a parent in a meeting called to discuss teen-age problems. The concerned father could see no need for counseling. "If people would just read the Bible, pray, and listen to good sermons," he stated emphatically, "there would be no need for counseling and counselors."

This viewpoint is shared by others, including some well-known Christians. Jimmy Swaggart once put it this way:

Now, let's look for a moment at the word "counseling." This has become the mainstay of efforts to help most people within our churches today. It used to be that the preaching of the Gospel performed this task. . . . No more. Counseling is now the great thruway that leads all to help and healing—be it pastoral or clinical counseling. . . . If individuals can't be pulled up out of the filth by the powerful and anointed preaching of the Word of God, there is little that can be done for them through personal counseling. . . . One of the truest statements ever made was this: "When people come asking for advice, they seldom want to hear the *truth*, they just want to receive *support* for what they've already decided!"[1]

This statement shows several misunderstandings about counseling. First, good counseling is never intended to replace good preaching. By teaching and example Jesus showed that preaching is an important part of the church's ministry. No committed Christian counselor would propose that preaching give way to counseling. Carefully prepared, Spirit-directed sermons reach and help many people, including those who also could benefit from counseling but would never go for help.

Second, it simply is not true that if people are untouched by preaching "there is little that can be done for them through personal counseling." Jesus spent many hours talking privately with the disciples and answering their questions, even though they often heard him preach. Modern evangelists often follow their preaching by inviting people to come forward in a meeting or to call a telephone number so they can talk with a counselor. Good preaching proclaims the Word of God publicly; good counseling applies the Word of God privately. Both may be abused, but both can also be used by the Holy Spirit to change lives. Sometimes one is effective when the other is not.

Third, whether or not they go for counseling, people who experience mental anguish need more than good preaching; they are helped when they feel part of a caring local church body. Surely the psychologist is right who stated that counseling between two isolated individuals is not nearly as effective as counseling that is backed up by church involvement. This involvement may include helpful preaching as well as support from warm, genuine, sensitive people who care.

There are other reasons why counseling is sometimes needed.

The Bible encourages counseling. Jesus, who spoke to the multitudes, didn't preach to Nicodemus, to the woman at the well, to Mary and Martha, to the person caught in adultery, or to the woman with the issue of blood. With these and many others he talked privately, wept, shared their hurts, gave encouragement and guided them as they coped with their problems. Sometimes he taught, confronted and called for repentance. At other times he listened, forgave and called for confession. He served food, washed feet, encouraged humility, drew pictures, asked questions, listened carefully, and often told stories that left people free to draw their own conclusions.[2]

Throughout the New Testament, personal helping is modeled and encouraged. Think, for example, of John's tender epistles, Paul's pastoral guidance to young Timothy, Peter's intensely practical letters, James's encouragement or Paul's sensitive letter to Philemon concerning Onesimus. Over fifty "one another" instructions are given to readers of the Scriptures. Most of these—bear one another's burdens, encourage one another, comfort one another, care for one another, pray for one another, serve one another in love, be kind to one another—are teachings that stimulate believers to help and counsel others.

Many people need counseling. It is naive to assume that all problems will be solved through biblical preaching alone. Some people never hear preaching. Some hear but don't listen. Some listen but are too distraught, sick, anguished, disoriented or confused to understand.

It is *not* "one of the truest statements ever made" that people who go for counseling only "want to receive support for what they've already decided." For some this probably is true, but few people, especially hurting people, are likely to spend time and energy and money going to a counselor who will support their prior decisions. More often, counselees come with a sincere desire to find answers to troublesome questions, solutions to persisting problems, guidance in making difficult decisions, relief from inhibiting emotions or habits, and help in coping with intensive stresses.

Sermons, seminars, self-help books and media appearances by pastors or professional counselors can all be helpful in combating despair, providing solace, giving insights and changing behavior. It is probable, however, that these public approaches to helping are most useful to people who are alert and calm enough to apply what they learn. When stresses become intense, many individuals are not able to apply what they hear. They need the personal guidance that comes from a sensitive counselor.

Helpers often benefit from counseling. This message is rarely mentioned in the counseling literature. We hope that counselees will benefit from counseling, but little is said about the personal benefits that can come to a sensitive and caring counselor who reaches out to others.

The Christian message is one of loving, forgiving, helping, doing good and caring. Individuals who think only about themselves and their own problems have a narrow focus of interest. Sometimes one of the best ways to help ourselves is to look for ways to encourage and help others. This can be a form of counseling that benefits both the one who gives and the one who receives.

The Bible instructs us to cast our cares and anxieties on the Lord, and promises in return that he will sustain and care for us (Ps 55:22;

1 Pet 5:7.) Sometimes this divine help comes through preaching. Sometimes it comes directly from the Holy Spirit as he brings comfort, often through the words of Scripture. Surely God also helps, at times, through the individual guidance of sensitive counselors.

God is sufficient and able to meet our needs. To go for counseling is not to deny this truth. The Scriptures and our own experiences give abundant evidence that God can, and does, work through capable, sensitive counselors. Often these counselors will listen, give encouragement, challenge thinking and employ a host of other techniques that are used both by Christian counselors and by those who are nonbelievers. Because they understand the things of the Spirit (1 Cor 2:14), Christian counselors will bring the added plus of spiritual sensitivity to the counseling session. But none of this implies that God is unable to meet human needs. On the contrary, the help that comes from caring counselors is one of the best ways by which our all-powerful God brings change and healing in times of need.

Why Go to Psychologists If They Never Help Anyone?

3

*A*CCORDING TO ONE RELIABLE ESTIMATE, MORE THAN FOUR THOUSAND INTER-view programs are broadcast daily throughout the United States and Canada.[1] Over a million guests appear every year. Occasionally this includes me.

Not long ago a man dialed a call-in radio program and said, "It makes no sense to me. Why would anyone go to a psychologist for counseling when psychologists never help anyone?" What are the facts?

1. Many people have high expectations about counseling. Perhaps some counselors have been guilty of creating expectations about their work that, though widely held, are not always valid.[2]

Many people have come to assume, for example, that there are hidden psychological explanations for most human behavior, and that professional counselors are experts who can unlock these inner mysteries and liberate people from their personal hang-ups. As a result, these people look for experts who can help them find self-understanding, greater affluence, freedom from anxiety and continual happiness.

Who is the expert that is supposed to help us find happiness? One psychologist's answer is sobering:

People who believe they are entitled to happiness tend to be receptive to almost anything that promises to relieve them of affliction and annoyance, deficiency and incompetence, or whatever else they believe is in the path of their feeling better. The bearing of crosses is not for them and neither is the acceptance of tragedy or of personal limitations. They want ways around such things. . . .

Counseling is one of the main places we go when we feel that we're not getting as much out of life as we should, that we're not experiencing as much joy, that we're not fulfilling our potential.[3]

Great expectations bring a lot of people to therapy, but sometimes we expect a lot more than any counselor can deliver.

2. *Many writers have presented dramatic criticisms of therapy.* Most begin with Hans Eysenck's 1952 conclusion that "roughly two-thirds of a group of neurotic patients will recover or improve to a marked extent within about two years of the onset of their illness, whether they are treated by means of psychotherapy or not.[4]

Some of therapy's critics are gentle and leave room for the possibility that counseling can be effective, at least under some circumstances. Other critics are more forceful in their evaluations. Psychotherapy, says one book, is "a distortion and a deceit based solely upon the testimonies and hopes of therapists and their clients. . . . The results of psychotherapy are both questionable and unpredictable."[5] Therapy, we read, is "a system supported by sparsity of proof."[6] It has been called a pseudoscience riddled with contradiction,[7] and part of a field that is insane and "literally a mess."[8]

These are serious charges. If psychotherapy and related forms of counseling are as harmful as these critics claim, then many people—including the lady on that call-in program—have good reason to be concerned.

3. Many researchers have done careful scientific studies to evaluate the effectiveness of therapy. Psychologist Allen Bergin, for example, reanalyzed Eysenck's data and showed that his oft-quoted findings are not accurate.[9] Eysenck imposed a set of standards on the data that "yielded the lowest possible improvement rates while being more lenient with the spontaneous remission data."[10] The widely quoted conclusion that two-thirds of neurotic patients will improve in two years without treatment is simply not right, Bergin discovered. It is a conclusion unsupported by research data.[11] Regrettably, however, Eysenck's erroneous results are quoted as fact by almost every critic of psychology and psychotherapy.

We do not have space to summarize the hundreds of psychotherapy research studies,[12] but a few of their conclusions are of special interest.

For example, there is now a consensus that psychotherapy is more effective than no therapy.[13] People who appear to get better by themselves are still getting help. Most often they turn to friends, informal counseling or self-help approaches similar to more formal therapy.[14]

There is evidence that the people who are harmed by therapy most often are the severely disturbed or those with counselors who themselves are maladjusted.[15]

There is no evidence that one school or theory of psychotherapy leads to better results than another.[16]

Long-term treatment does not appear to be more effective than briefer treatment approaches.[17]

Research evidence is still being collected. It would be irresponsible to deny the weaknesses and problems in psychotherapy, but, based on what we know thus far, it is also irresponsible to dismiss psychotherapy as a pseudoscience riddled with contradictions and confusion. Such a conclusion is clear bias, not supported by research.

4. Many benefits can come from therapy, in spite of its weaknesses. According to one review of the research, therapy can help people feel better. As a result, many people don't feel as hopeless, alone, overwhelmed or unable to cope with life. "While it is overpromoted, overused, and overevaluated, it can be beneficial when used prudently, with clear understanding of its powers, limitations, and risks."[18]

If you decide to go for counseling, don't assume that all therapists are incompetent. Many are both competent and helpful.

Don't assume, either, that all therapists are capable and competent. There *are* ineffective and emotionally disturbed counselors offering their services. Regrettably, this includes some who call themselves Christians.

How do you find a counselor who really can help? Recommendations from local medical or psychological societies are probably not always the best ways to locate a good counselor. Try instead to find a friend, work associate, Christian leader or respected professional who can make a recommendation. Don't be afraid to shop around, to ask a counselor about his or her training and approach, and to seek someone with whom you feel some personal rapport. If possible, try to find someone whose values and beliefs are similar to yours. Counselees are more likely to get better and to experience personal growth when their values are similar to those of the therapist.[19]

I wish there had been time to discuss all of this with the man on that call-in program.

But he hung up.

Should a Christian Ever Go to A Non-Christian Counselor?

*T*HE LADY WHO CALLED WAS DISTRESSED, AND IT WASN'T HARD TO UNDERSTAND why.

Her teen-age son professed to be a Christian and attended church regularly. She and her husband had discovered, however, that the boy was heavily involved with drugs, and on the day of the phone call he had made a serious suicide attempt. The school was concerned and had recommended a local psychiatrist who wanted to hospitalize the young man and begin immediate treatment.

"Is it OK for a Christian to be treated by a non-Christian psychiatrist?" the mother asked.

This is a common question, and I usually respond with the same answer: Whenever possible, it is preferable for Christians to seek help from competent Christian counselors.

One research study found that conservative Christians have six fears about secular counselors. Christians fear that the secular counselor will (1) ignore spiritual concerns, (2) assume that spiritual beliefs and experiences are evidences of pathology or merely psychological, (3) not understand spiritual language and ideas (see 1 Cor 2:14), (4) assume that religious counselees share common secular views on issues such as premarital sex or divorce, (5) recommend so-called therapeutic activities—such as sexual experimentation—that Christians consider immoral or (6) make assumptions, draw conclusions and give recommendations that are antibiblical.[1] Conservative Christians clearly prefer like-minded counselors. Believers fear that in secular counseling, their values might be changed, weakened, laughed at or misunderstood.

Are these fears justified? Is it possible that religious beliefs really will be undermined in counseling?

The research findings are not conclusive, and much depends on both the counselee and the counselor. Nevertheless, some scientific evidence indicates that counselees *do* change their values in counseling. When counseling is successful, the counselee's values—including religious values—become more like those of the counselor.[2] According to one study of group counseling, "psychotherapy may have its greatest effect on attitudes of a philosophical nature dealing with ethics and religion."[3]

One sensitive Christian psychologist has studied and summarized many of the research reports. He freely admits that the conclusions are only tentative, at present, but his summary is enlightening:

Many researchers have investigated the fear and concerns of religious clients about attending counseling with a counselor who has different values. Clients prefer counselors who have values similar to their own. Yet, extant research indicates that once counseling has begun, clients are apparently less able to discriminate counselors with similar values and counselors with dissimilar values. Research is needed to test this implication directly. There is also evidence that once counseling is begun, the client's religious values are likely to become more like the counselor's. Thus, some of the client's fears are substantiated by research. The client should select a counselor whose religious values

_____ 31 _____

are admired. Other fears (e.g., that the client will be misunderstood or undiagnosed) have not been supported.[4]

At this point it would be easiest to end the chapter, conclude that secular counselors should be avoided and move on to the next question.

Regrettably, however, one big problem remains. We may agree that, whenever possible, it is preferable for Christians to seek help from competent Christian counselors. But what do we do when it is not possible to get help from a believer because no Christian counselors are available? Where does one go for help when local Christian counselors are known to be incompetent? Do we tell a concerned mother to send her suicidal teen-age son to an untrained and inexperienced counselor who is Christian but who may have no understanding of adolescent suicide, the nature of habitual drug use or the physiological aspects of drug addiction?

Frequently it simply is not possible to find a competent Christian counselor. At such times we must settle on the most acceptable alternative available. In making this decision it can be helpful to ask some basic questions.

What is the problem? Sometimes the problem has little or nothing to do with values. It may be, for example, primarily medical, educational or vocational. In such cases, the counselor and counselee may never discuss religion or personal morals. The non-Christian physician can be effective in treating disease or in changing a chemical imbalance that might be causing a Christian's depression. A specialist in learning disabilities can make a significant impact on Christian or non-Christian students who are failing in school. A guidance counselor can give aptitude tests or vocational suggestions, leaving the Christian counselee to determine how this relates to finding and doing God's will. When problems are largely value-free, the Christian has less need to seek a Christian who can give counseling.

Who are the available counselors? It would be highly inaccurate to assume that most non-Christian counselors are like vultures, ready to pounce on the Christian's faith in an attempt to ridicule it, tear it apart and destroy it. On the contrary, secular counselors frequently recognize the mental health value of religion and seek to strengthen rather than weaken the counselee's religious faith. Some secular helpers may not understand Christian language or ways of thinking, and many will not agree with the Christian's beliefs and values. Nevertheless, many consider it both unethical and bad counseling technique to undermine the counselee's belief system.

There is evidence, however, that secular professional counselors, as a group, are personally not very religious.[5] Undoubtedly many are opposed to religion and seek to free counselees from beliefs that the counselors consider harmful.

How can one know if this is the counselor's attitude? It isn't always easy to tell where a counselor stands, but there is no harm in asking before you commit time and money to any treatment program. If a counselor objects to your question about his or her attitudes toward religion, this in itself may be a signal warning you to be careful.

What is the reputation of the counselor or treatment program? The best advertisements for a school are the people who graduate. Can the same be said for a counselor? Try to find a counselee or former counselee who can give a perspective on the counselor's competence and attitudes toward religion. Fellow believers in the local church can also give guidance, but try not to make a decision based on hearsay and unsubstantiated rumor.

Christians who believe in the power of prayer agree that our God is able to lead us to the person or persons, Christian or secular, who can best give help in times of need. That confidence in divine leading and in the power of prayer can take away much anxiety about finding the best counselor.

This was the message I gave the lady with the suicidal son. She and her husband prayed about the situation and discussed it with their pastor, their son and the school officials. When all things were considered this Christian family chose to admit the young man to a secular residential treatment program.

I don't think their decision was wrong.

Should Christians Take Therapeutic Drugs?

5

ITS BEEN CALLED THE DRUGGING OF AMERICA, THE MAINSTAY OF WESTERN PSY-chiatric therapy, the great escape hatch.

Every year literally tons of mood-altering drugs are taken by people who want to avoid insomnia, escape anxiety, rise out of depression and calm tensions. It is difficult to get out of a psychiatrist's office without some kind of minor tranquilizer,[1] and even general practitioners write literally millions of prescriptions annually for what one writer has called "mind candy, . . . pills for anxiety."[2]

Psychotherapeutic drugs have revolutionized psychiatry and the entire field of counseling. I made my first visit to a mental hospital in the 1950s when I was a student. Patients were hollering, hallucinating, moving about in agitation, sometimes curled up in catatonic fetal positions on the floor and often tightly confined in straitjackets that restricted their movements and tendencies to be violent. Only a few years later, the hospitals were cleaner, less chaotic, calmer and with far fewer patients. Because of the new medications, many previously confined psychotic people had been released and at last were able to function with help outside the hospital.

Even with their many benefits, however, the widespread use of psychotherapeutic drugs has raised questions among Christians and others.

Are drugs overprescribed and overused? Psychiatrist Garth Wood is among those who answer yes. Most physicians, he suggests, lack the time, inclination and training to deal with psychological worries in their patients. It is much easier to prescribe a tablet that will dull the symptoms and keep people from having to face the causes of their distress. By taking tranquilizing drugs, individuals do little to solve their own problems, but they solve "those of the doctor who saves time and energy by prescribing" drugs, and they solve those of manufacturers who profit from increasing drug sales.[3]

Is it fair to put all the blame on doctors and drug manufacturers? Probably not. We live in a society where people expect instant relief from tension, unhappiness, worry and discouragement. We flock to doctors asking for pills to take away anxiety. Many physicians feel ill at ease discussing their patients' psychological or life problems, so they give the requested prescriptions and everyone is happy. Since nonmedical counselors cannot dispense medications, they often encourage their counselees to get drugs from physicians, and everybody feels better.

Do drugs prevent people from facing their problems? In a widely acclaimed and thought-provoking book, psychiatrist M. Scott Peck begins with three simple words that in his opinion are among the greatest of all truths: *Life is difficult.*[4]

This truth is not popular in our society. We have come to believe that happiness is a basic human right, that we should always feel positive and worry free, that discontent is unnatural, and that guilt is unhealthy and inhibiting. Whenever they feel frustrated, worried, fed up, bored or sad, many people turn to self-help books or mood-changing drugs to "steady the nerves" and bring a feeling of relief.

Peck and others remind us, however, that problems and discouragements are a natural part of living. They don't go away by themselves or because medications dull their pain. Instead, problems exist to try us, test us and teach us. When they are faced squarely and honestly, they help us grow mentally and spiritually. This message appears occasionally in psychiatry books,[5] but it was stated powerfully by the apostle James many years ago. "Consider it pure joy, my brothers, whenever you face trials of many kinds, because you know that the testing of your faith develops perseverance. Perseverance must finish its work so that you may be mature and complete, not lacking anything" (Jas 1:2-3).

Since psychotherapeutic drugs first appeared in the 1950s, there has been debate about whether taking drugs removes the person's motivation for solving problems. To date, there is no solid research support to indicate that this happens.[6] Even when they are taking medications, many people still work on their problems. To do so can bring greater self-respect and more permanent relief.

Do psychotherapeutic drugs serve any useful purpose? As researchers accumulate more data about mental illness, it is becoming clearer that many forms of psychopathology have a biological basis. Intense anxiety, for example, was once thought to be solely a psychological disturbance or evidence of a spiritual lack of trust. It is now well established that severe anxiety, including devastating panic attacks, often has a biological basis. Sometimes this chemically induced "anxiety disease" may have a genetic cause.[7] Present research suggests that the best treatment may be a combination of drugs and behavior therapy. Surely there are few people who would deny that medication is a great benefit in such cases.

Medication can also be beneficial when the problems are less severe and the causes less clearly biological. Often a mild tranquilizer or antidepressant will calm a troubled mind and free the individual to work at facing and solving problems. On occasion, taking an antianxiety drug will help people feel more relaxed so they can do things like public speaking that would be difficult or impossible otherwise. When taken under the direction of a physician who is careful and knowledgeable, such medication can be helpful.

Sometimes we forget that many apparent "emotional" problems really result from physical disorders. Attention Deficit Disorder (ADD), for example, is relatively common especially among children. The symptoms are largely psychological—hyperactivity, inability to concentrate, distractibility, nervous mannerisms, impulsiveness, and mood swings—but the cause appears to be physical. It results, most often, from a genetically acquired malfunctioning of the central nervous system, and it is best treated with drugs. What at first appears to be an emotional, spiritual or discipline problem really is a physical problem. Psychiatric textbooks include numerous other examples. Chemical, neurological and medical conditions often create physically based emotional problems that are best treated by medication.

Can psychotherapeutic drugs lead to addiction? When used in high dosages for prolonged periods of time, many medications can become physiologically and psychologically addicting. A report from England indicated that in a population of 55 million people, 21 million tranquilizer prescriptions were written during a recent one-year period. That's one prescription for every 2.6 people. A government estimate suggests that 100,000 British people are to some extent addicted to tranquilizing drugs.[8] Might the situation be as bad or worse on this side of the Atlantic?

It probably is true that some people cannot function without consistent use of medications, but it is likely that fewer abuses would occur if physicians stopped giving open-ended prescriptions and started monitoring drug use more carefully.

Are the benefits of mood-changing drugs sometimes exaggerated? Members of the American Psychiatric Association were jolted at a recent meeting when they heard initial results of a $10 million government study of psychotherapy. When depressed patients who had been treated by drugs were compared with other people who had not been given any drugs but who had received cognitive or interpersonal therapy, all groups improved equally. The drug-treatment patients got quicker results, but after several weeks the therapy patients caught up. In all groups serious symptoms of depression were eliminated in more than half the patients. (Perhaps I should add that 29% of the patients in a separate control group also lost their symptoms, even though they got no treatment at all.[9] Apparently the benefits of psychotherapeutic drugs *can* be exaggerated.

Why are some Christians resistant to the use of psychotherapeutic drugs? Some people are willing to take aspirin or other medication to deal with physical illnesses, but they feel it is wrong or a sign of weakness to take mood-altering drugs. Perhaps there are those who feel that taking such drugs is to admit that one is mentally ill. Some may fear that drugs will oversedate, make them more vulnerable to a counselor's suggestions, or dull thinking—despite evidence that this is highly unlikely when the drug dosage is mild and carefully monitored by a physician. Many believers may forget or fail to understand that drugs are used frequently to treat physical conditions that have been causing emotional and other psychological symptoms.

Among Christians, a greater resistance to psychotherapeutic medication probably comes from those who believe that drug use is a sign of spiritual weakness. Many feel that Christians shouldn't have overwhelming struggles and psychological problems. When stresses arise, these people feel that prayer, trusting the Lord and meditation on Scripture are the only Christian ways to cope with anxiety. When Jesus was on the cross, he didn't take the drug that was offered, so why should his followers cop out with medications?

The dedication of such people is to be admired. The Scriptures do provide guidance for coping with many of life's problems, and we are instructed to cast our anxieties on the Lord (1 Pet 5:7), to bear each other's burdens (Gal 6:2), to cast our problems on Christ (Mt 11:28-30) and to pray with the expectation that our requests will be granted (Mt 21:22).

Even in Jesus' time, however, the God-given wisdom of professional healers was not dismissed. If the Lord has allowed us to discover new chemical tools to counteract the biological bases of human problems and to help us cope temporarily with the stresses of life, are these necessarily wrong? When drugs distract us from facing problems or prevent us from seeking biblically based solutions to our struggles, then using them is not right. But psychotherapeutic medications can help us relax so that we can think more clearly. Their use is neither wrong nor an indication that we lack faith.

Why Is Professional Counseling So Expensive?

*P*ROFESSIONAL PEOPLE-HELPING IS A BIG BUSINESS—ESPECIALLY IN AMERICA. Thousands of psychiatrists, an estimated forty-five thousand clinical psychologists and approximately sixty thousand clinical social workers do therapy for a fee. Their ranks are swelled by university professors, pastoral counselors, self-styled advice givers and even lay people who don't claim to be therapists but often give counseling in return for payment. One writer estimates that there are half a million professional and paraprofessional counselors in this country—all part of a "psychotherapy industry" that may take in as much as $17 billion annually.[1]

Payment for counseling ranges from a few dollars paid to students in training to the $150 or more that some psychiatrists charge for a half-hour consultation. According to one recent report, the average psychiatrist's fee is $90 for each fifty-minute session. Psychologists receive an average of $60 per hour. Clinical social workers usually charge less.[2]

Do the buyers of counseling get what they pay for?

This question has been debated for decades. Since Freud's time some professional therapists have argued that when people pay for treatment, they are more involved, more inclined to value the counseling and willing to work harder to get better. Perhaps most people believe that we get what we pay for. If therapy comes from a professional who charges high fees, it must be worth more than the free counseling available from pastors or others who charge little or nothing. This assumption may have permitted counselors to overcharge for their services. Thus far, however, we don't have research evidence either to support or refute such a conclusion.[3]

One psychologist adds another piece to the payment puzzle. Often, he argues, there aren't enough paying clients to fill the consulting rooms of all the therapists. To solve this problem, some therapists find themselves involved in "the selling of therapy."[4] This isn't blatant manipulation. Most therapists probably haven't even noticed what they are doing. Subtly, however, they convince people that their lives could be better, that therapy will help them and that "a few more sessions" would be a wise investment in their future happiness and stability. Soon people who aren't sick are willingly paying to get better.

All of this costs money. Some would say too much money.[5] "How can counselors, including Christian counselors, say they are helping people when they charge such outlandish fees?" one student asked. Is professional counseling only for the rich or the heavily insured?

Let us begin to answer by agreeing that some counseling is overpriced. There are therapists, including Christians, who charge outrageous fees. I know of no research to support those who rationalize that counselees have more confidence in counselors who work in palatial offices and demand high payment. Some fees appear to be based mostly on the counselor's greed—and greed is wrong.

We should recognize, however, that counselors' fees are not always as extreme as they appear. General practitioners and pediatricians charge less per consultation, but they see a large number of patients each hour. Lawyers, business consultants, optometrists and numerous other professionals charge fees that are within the same range, and often higher, than those of a trained counselor.

When we write a check to pay for these services, it is easy to think that the whole fee goes into the professional's pocket. That isn't true. Office rent, telephone and electric bills, the cost of a twenty-four-hour answering service, the receptionist's salary, billing expenses and other overhead costs eat up much of the fee. Because of the increase in lawsuits, liability insurance for professionals has risen to exorbitant levels. In addition, it is expensive to belong to professional organizations, to take refresher courses and to subscribe to journals that keep the counselor updated. Whenever an appointment is canceled, the expenses continue but the therapist doesn't get paid for that hour. Too many people don't pay their bills, so this adds more expense for the therapist (and for the counselees who do pay.)

Does this sound like a hard-luck story? It is meant instead to show that professional counselors aren't always paid as highly as it might seem.

And nonprofessionals aren't really free. Pastoral counselors, for example, usually don't charge a fee, but somebody—usually the church members—pay the counselor's salary, office expenses and overhead costs.

In pondering the issue of fees, we can learn much from the apostle Paul. In the early church, traveling teachers and evangelists went from place to place living off the generosity of others. More than anyone else, Paul had reason to be supported in such a way, but he resisted. He worked to support himself. He preached "free of charge" (2 Cor 11:7). He warned against church leaders who pursue "dishonest gain" (1 Tim 3:8) or are motivated by "selfish ambition" (Phil 2:3) and "greed" (1 Thess 2:5; Eph 5:3). "Unlike so many," Paul wrote to the Corinthians, "we do not peddle the word of God for profit" (2 Cor 2:17).

Surely there is nothing wrong with workmen, including counselors, charging a fair fee for their services (Mt 10:10). Even when friends or church leaders are available, some people prefer to talk with a professional,[6] and many problems are of such intensity that the trained, paid counselor is the most available experienced helper. Christian professionals have a responsibility before God to set a fee structure that is fair to their needs without being exorbitant.

Critics of high fees sometimes forget that many counselors, including many non-Christians, do a great deal of counseling for little or no pay. People with lower incomes often are seen for reduced fees, and few counselors would ignore the pleas of a desperate person who needed help but couldn't pay.

Some counselors may be money-grabbers who line their pockets by charging fees that are too high. There are people like that in all professions, but it isn't true of the majority. When everything is considered, including counselor costs, most fees are neither as high nor as exorbitant as some critics would have us believe.

Are Lay Counselors as Effective as Professionals?

MY FRIEND MARK RECENTLY GOT HIS DOCTORATE IN PSYCHOLOGY.

He is bright, young, enthusiastic, excited about his profession, anxious to help people and convinced that counseling others is an effective way to serve Christ.

Mark is also convinced that nonprofessionals should not try to be counselors. "They cause a lot of harm," he protested over lunch recently. "Untrained 'counselors' often fail to understand the complexities of human behavior. They give simplistic advice, aren't skilled enough to spot serious pathology, overlook physical causes for problems, rarely think about making referrals to a trained professional, and frequently make matters worse instead of better."

There is some truth in my friend's observations. Apparently, however, he is not aware of the accumulating research that contrasts trained counselors with those who have little or no training.

Several years ago, a researcher at the University of Southern Illinois reviewed forty-two studies that compared professional counselors with untrained helpers. The findings were "consistent and provocative. Paraprofessionals achieve clinical outcomes equal to or significantly better than those obtained by professionals."[1]

In one study, for example, highly experienced counselors treated fifteen college students who suffered from neurotic depression and anxiety. A similar group was treated by college professors who had no counselor training and no special knowledge of psychiatry. The group treated by the professors did as well as those counseled by the professionals. According to the researcher's report, "The study, on the whole, lent no support to the major hypothesis that . . . the technical skills of professional psychotherapists produce measurably better therapeutic change."[2]

One critic of psychology, a medical doctor with training in psychiatry, responded with an interesting comparison: "Imagine the same being true of surgery. A controlled study at a major university showing that actors were as good at brain surgery as neurosurgeons. Consider the outcry that such a study might cause. Nothing would ever be the same again. But in the weird world of psychotherapy, the research sinks without a trace. So what that laymen do it as well as professionals. Let's ignore it, and carry on as before, pocketing the money and hoping no one will notice."[3]

Is it fair to compare counseling with brain surgery? The doctor who did this also admitted that about eighty per cent of medical training is of little use since most of the physician's work deals with coughs and colds, aches and pains, or other ailments that could be as well treated by lay people.

But lay people can't do brain surgery. That's a job for specialists.

In a similar way, perhaps it is true that lay people can effectively recognize and treat the large majority of personality problems and psychiatric illnesses. Maybe we could even agree that an intelligent layman might be able to learn how to help most people after only a long weekend of training.[4] Clearly there is evidence that for most problems, lay people can counsel as well as or better than the professionals.

But is their success rate as good with the more serious problems? Do we need specialists like my friend Mark to do the psychological equivalent of brain surgery?

However you might answer, some conclusions about lay counseling are clear.

Lay counseling can and does help people. In a still-valid research report published in 1968, conclusive evidence was presented to show that "with or without training . . . the patients of lay counselors do as well or better than the patients of professional counselors." This was true in studies with both hospitalized and nonhospitalized neuropsychiatric patients, with both adults and children, and with normal people who were "situationally distressed."[5]

Why is this true? Some have suggested that many professionals are too busy to really care about people, too worried about professional image to get really involved with their counselees, or so distracted with concerns about technique and theory that they are less able to relate to the people who come for help. Perhaps professionals see so many counselees that it isn't possible always to keep alert and bring constant freshness to counseling. Laypersons, by contrast, are freer to focus attention on only one or two people, so the counseling can be more intense, less rushed, more caring and less like an assembly line.

Lay counseling is not the panacea for all human problems. Before we dismiss all professional psychologists and turn counseling over to lay people, it should be mentioned that evaluating lay counseling is as difficult, and often as inconclusive, as studying professional, pastoral and various other types of Christian counseling.

Sometimes depression, anxiety, learning disabilities and similar problems are assumed to have psychological or spiritual causes, but the basic cause is physical and calls for a physical treatment. Only medical people are professionally qualified and legally entitled to treat such illnesses. Well-trained nonmedical counselors who understand psychopathology are aware of physical issues and more inclined to encourage counselees to get competent medical examinations and treatment.

Professionals know the ease with which counselors—especially inexperienced and untrained counselors—can misinterpret symptoms, give insensitive guidance or advice, be manipulated by counselees, or fail to understand the complexities of abnormal behavior. Professionals, of course, can make all these errors as well, but the trained counselor is more alert to spotting and avoiding such dangers.

Lay counseling should be an important part of the church's work and ministry. It has often been suggested that there would be no need for professional counselors if church members were consistently bearing one another's burdens.

In theory, this is true. The support, challenge, love and guidance that can come from involvement with a caring body of fellow believers can have therapeutic value unequaled anyplace else. In reality, however, we must admit that most people don't attend church, and many churches are not caring or therapeutic. It is worth the effort to create caring church bodies, but until we have more of them, people with problems will seek other ways to cope with the pressures of an increasingly stressful society. When the pressure gets intense, most people turn to professional counselors.

Garth Wood is a physician who makes no claim to be religious. In a thought-provoking and provocative book, *The Myth of Neurosis: Overcoming the Illness Excuse,* he argues that much of what we call mental illness and neurosis is really evidence of common problems in living. By calling these problems "neurotic," we are able to talk about them with a professional, blame someone else for their existence, find excuses for their persistence and avoid taking responsibility for their solution. Instead, says Wood, we should admit that most of our problems could be solved by discussing them with a friend and taking action to overcome them. Even with this strong defense of lay helping, however, Wood admits that professionals will always be needed to treat severe mental illness. Specialists are still needed to do the psychological equivalent of brain surgery!

My friend Mark would agree. Because of his professional training, he has counseling skills, insights and understanding that he might not otherwise have. Mark is a good counselor who is a specialist in his field. But an impressive body of research shows what Mark probably does not want to hear: *Not all*, but much, of what the professional counselor does can be done equally well or better by lay people with little or no training.

PART TWO
Questions about Christian Counseling

What Is Unique about Christian Counseling?

*T*HERE IS NO WAY TO PROVE IT.

It's only a hunch.

I hope it isn't true.

But my conversations with Christian counselors over the years have left me with the uncomfortable impression that most of them don't counsel in ways much different from those of their secular colleagues.

I encountered this with a class of military chaplains I taught recently. "There is no unique Christian surgery," one of the class members stated. "There is no unique Christian auto mechanics or cooking. Why should we assume that anything is unique about Christian counseling?"

The answer begins with the recognition that God, through the Bible, has given us what we need to know for living this life and for avoiding corruption (2 Pet 1:3-4). Nowhere does the Bible claim to be a counseling text or a self-help handbook for happiness, but the Scriptures do contain hundreds of principles for living. The Bible is "useful to teach us what is true and to make us realize what is wrong in our lives; it straightens us out and helps us do what is right. It is God's way of making us well prepared at every point, fully equipped to do good to everyone" (2 Tim 3:16-17 Living Bible). The Bible teaches us about God and the universe, gives comfort and encouragement, and shows through many practical examples how past generations have coped with the stresses of life.

Some Christian counselors believe it is unethical in a counseling session to mention religion, talk about God or quote the Bible—unless the counselee raises these issues first. One of my former students recently quit a secure and well-paying counseling job because the secular agency for which he worked did not permit discussion of religion in the counseling session. The counselor respected his employer's policies and recognized that government-sponsored institutions cannot condone anything that looks like proselytism. Nevertheless, he felt like a doctor with a relevant, powerful, widely accepted, long-used approach to treatment who was not permitted to mention or use it unless it was suggested by the patient.

There are numerous Christian approaches to counseling, but each has unique assumptions, unique goals and unique methods.[1]

Unique assumptions. Every approach to counseling—secular or Christian—begins with an underlying set of presuppositions.[2] These assumptions influence counseling whether the counselor is aware of them or not. Although the assumptions may differ from one person to another, depending on the counselor's theological beliefs, Christian counselors tend to have unique assumptions about God, the universe, human beings, truth, pathology and guilt.

Most Christian counselors believe that *God* is eternal, sovereign, omnipresent, all-knowing, powerful and intimately acquainted with each person in the world. God exists in three persons—Father, Son and Holy Spirit—and cares about individual people. Secular counseling approaches say little about God, sometimes criticize those who believe, and tend to assume he is nonexistent or uninvolved in human concerns.

Concerning the *universe,* Christians believe that God created it, ultimately controls it and currently holds everything together (Heb 1:1-3). The secular counselor, in contrast, usually assumes that humans are valuable, but many would agree with Fromm that we are "alone in a universe indifferent to our fate."

The Bible states that *human beings* were created in the divine image, but we fell into sin and thus alienated ourselves from God. Because God values and loves us, he sent Jesus Christ, his Son, to die for sinful human beings and to make eternal salvation possible for those who believe in him (Jn 3:16). We are not rescued automatically or against our wills. Salvation comes to those who deliberately acknowledge Jesus Christ as Lord and put their lives under his control (Rom 3:22-24; 10:9; Eph 2:8). Secular counseling says nothing definitive about salvation, ultimate human destiny or one's relationship with God.

Concerning what we know about *truth* (philosophers call this *epistemology),* most Christians believe that the Holy Spirit teaches and guides. He does this especially through the pages of God's inspired Word, the Bible, our infallible guide of faith and conduct. We also learn through reading, interaction with others, logical reasoning, empirical research and other means—but no conclusion can be accepted as true or valid unless it is consistent with the teachings of Scripture. The secular counselor would likely dismiss the Bible's relevance and proclaim that human reason and scientific findings are the basis for making ultimate decisions.

Most Christians would agree that all human problems, including *psychopathology,* arise ultimately from sin in the human race and at least sometimes from the counselee's personal sin. Christians differ in their views concerning the extent to which personal responsibility and environmental influences cause problems. Secular counselors also debate the responsibility-environmental causation issue, but almost none accepts the idea that sin, as rebellion against God, is an important cause of pathology.

Another major difference between Christian and secular counselors concerns their views about *guilt* and *forgiveness*. In secular counseling, painful experiences and mistakes can only be talked about, "forgotten" or used as learning experiences. Christians, in contrast, believe that we can be forgiven by God and can learn to forgive others.

Many common terms—love, peace, self-control, joy, sexual fulfillment, security, self-esteem, spiritual growth, sin, purity, to name a few—are used by both secular and Christian counselors, but often with different meanings. This can create communication difficulties.

Unique goals. Counseling books often include similar lists of counseling goals: to help counselees change behavior, attitudes, values and/or perceptions; to teach skills, including social skills; to encourage the recognition and expression of emotion; to give support in times of need; to teach responsibility; to instill insight; to guide as decisions are made; to help counselees mobilize inner and environmental resources in times of crisis; to teach future problem-solving skills; and to increase counselee competence and foster personal growth.

The Christian counselor accepts most or all of these goals, but in addition he or she should seek opportunities to—

☐ present the gospel message and encourage counselees to commit their lives to Jesus Christ

☐ stimulate spiritual growth

☐ encourage the confession of sin and the experience of divine forgiveness

☐ model Christian standards, attitudes and lifestyle

☐ stimulate counselees to develop values and live lives based on biblical teaching, instead of living in accordance with relativistic humanistic standards

These goals are not pursued in rigid ways that are insensitive to the counselee's values and place in life. The goals are not intended to push religion on clients or to manipulate people unethically. Nevertheless, the Christian who ignores such issues also risks building counseling on limited secular approaches, stifling his or her own beliefs, and compartmentalizing life into the sacred and the secular.

Christian counseling shares many of the goals of secular counseling, but, in addition, the Christian's goals include a concern about the counselee's relationship to Jesus Christ and acceptance of Christian values.[3]

Unique techniques. It has been suggested that all therapeutic techniques have at least four common features. They seek to arouse belief that help is possible, to correct harmful thinking and beliefs, to help people accept themselves as persons of worth and to teach individuals how to get along better in this world. To accomplish these ends, counselors use such basic techniques as listening, showing interest, trying to understand, and at times giving direction. Most Christian counselors have no problems with the four counseling features, or with most use the standard techniques that characterize all counseling.

The secular counselor is inclined to choose techniques on the basis of their pragmatic value. If a technique works, it is used, providing no one is harmed physically or emotionally. The Christian likewise selects techniques that are known to work, but in addition the Christian tests techniques against the authority of biblical teachings and (for many believers) against the conclusions of Christian theology.

In practice, therefore, the Christian (a) accepts and uses many standard counseling techniques, (b) refuses on moral, biblical or theological grounds to use some techniques used by secular counselors and (c) may use some techniques that secular counselors avoid—like prayer, reading the Bible, gentle confrontation with Christian truths, or encouraging counselees to become involved with a local church.

In terms of assumptions, goals and techniques, therefore, Christian counseling is often similar to secular counseling, but in many respects the two are—or should be—different. In many ways, Christian counseling is similar to discipling, but the effective Christian counselor brings additional knowledge and skills about interpersonal communication and emotional disorders.

It may be true that there is nothing uniquely Christian about surgery, auto mechanics or cooking. But that isn't true about counseling. Christian counseling should include much that is unique.

Is There a Spiritual Way to Counsel That Is Better Than the Psychological Way?

War is never pleasant or easy.

A lot of young Americans discovered this in a personal way when they were separated from their families and transported to the steamy jungles of South Vietnam. The war there was against an intensely dangerous guerrilla-backed force that often could not be seen or recognized. Many of the North Americans didn't know why they were so far from home, facing life-threatening situations and following orders to kill. Newspapers and letters revealed that the war was a source of great controversy in the United States and elsewhere. Even members of Congress wondered if this conflict was necessary for national defense or for the maintenance of world freedom.

It is not surprising that many Vietnam veterans tried to forget the war after it was all over. But that was not easy. The emotional pain persisted, and years after the war's end veterans are still appearing at counseling centers with complaints of mental turmoil, anxiety, tension and guilt.

In an interview, one counselor who works with veterans told about his work. "Our traditional psychiatric methods don't seem to be working with these veterans," the counselor said. "We encourage them to talk about their feelings, to admit their frustrations and to face their guilt, but they seem to need something more. They almost need a priest who will listen to their confessions and help them find forgiveness. Professional counseling is helpless in situations like this."

I thought about that interview when I read a book that contrasts "the psychological way" to counsel with "the spiritual way."[1] Written by two Christians, this book argues that psychotherapy—the psychological way—is an ineffective, false, antibiblical, destructive, deceptive, pseudoscientific new religion filled with "unproven ideas and abstract solutions."[2] It may be accepted and used by well-meaning people, the authors argue, but the church "does not need psychotherapy. . . . It has dishonestly usurped the ministry of the cure of souls and it distorts any form of Christianity to which it attaches itself."[3]

This is not an isolated viewpoint. As we have seen in earlier chapters, others agree that there are dangers in psychotherapy. Some believers are convinced that, for Christians, any problem that might be treated by psychological counseling could be better handled "by biblical counsel within the body of Christ."[4] The spiritual way of counseling is not only assumed to be better than the psychological way; it is presented as the only effective way to counsel.

Most Christians probably would agree with the following discussion of spiritual-biblical counseling:

At no time do we wish to give the impression that biblical counseling can be reduced to formulas. Those who counsel by formulas will fail. . . . True biblical counseling is . . . a creative, spiritual process involving a person who needs help and another person who will come alongside as God's channel of mercy and truth. . . . Each person who comes to counseling is unique, and God will minister in a unique way to that individual. The Scriptures and the Holy Spirit provide an infinite number of possible applications of truth to be ministered in love to each person in each situation. The biblical counselor attempts to be sensitive to the individual and to the Holy Spirit as he discusses or demonstrates biblical principles. If one were to take a biblical principle and apply it without regard for the counselee's readiness to receive or without being in harmony with God's work in a person's life, then even biblical principles may lead to disaster. It is possible to use the Bible and be wrong, and it is possible to quote the Bible and interfere with the work of God. Therefore, biblical counseling is a spiritual activity that combines the Word of God and the work of the Holy Spirit through one who is called to counsel and to one who will receive it.[5]

Must we conclude from this that there is a spiritual way to counsel that competes with and is superior to an inferior, ineffective, psychological way to give help? Such a statement sounds good but is too simplistic.

First, there is not just *one* psychological way and *one* spiritual way to counsel. Both psychological and Christian counseling have a variety of approaches, some of which disagree with others. As we have seen, the psychological ways are not as consistently ineffective as the critics maintain; and, as the above quotation notes, even biblical ways can lead to disaster if they are applied without sensitivity and care.

Second, it is not possible to put these two approaches into completely separate categories that can then be lined up against each other. The various secular and Christian approaches overlap and use many of the same techniques. Both emphasize listening, for example. Both stress counselor sensitivity and expressions of caring. Both may emphasize the importance of counselee motivation, facing responsibility, gaining insight, changing behavior, or learning to think differently. Some counselors in both camps emphasize love, forgiveness, support from a church group or even spiritual growth.[6] When the two camps are lined up against each other in an artificial way, many people are led to believe that there will be no overlap in terms of goals or methods. In fact, however, there is a lot of overlap.

Third, the two-way approach sometimes gives the erroneous impression that secular counseling has nothing of value to offer, that spiritual approaches are completely unique and effective, and that any good technique "discovered" by secular therapists really was in the Bible from the beginning.[7] These conclusions have not been demonstrated and probably are not valid.

Even so, Christians must agree that a "reflective knowledge of Scriptures along with a compassionate heart can, under the guidance of the Spirit, be used to uncover the root cause of problems that elude a purely psychological approach."[8] In spite of their many insights and helpful techniques, secular approaches often fail to explain behavior or adequately help people like those Vietnam veterans who needed to know about divine forgiveness. The biblical teachings on love, guilt, spiritual renewal, peace, joy, self-control, encouragement, sin and personal salvation, for example, *are* unique and need to be shared sensitively by spiritually alert counselors who know the Scriptures and seek to walk with God. The committed Christian counselor is well aware of the importance of praying for and sometimes with counselees, of sharing truths from Scripture at times and of encouraging people to find support in a local body of believers.

But it is confusing, potentially harmful and invalid to propose that there is one psychological way that deals with the "cure of minds," one spiritual way that deals with the "cure of souls," and no overlap.[9]

Counseling is more complex than that.

Does Christian Counseling Always Work?

*T*HERE ARE FEW THINGS I HATE MORE THAN BUYING A CAR. MOST CARS ARE TOO expensive. I tend to distrust car salesmen. And since I know nothing about automobile engines, I can't evaluate the vehicle's mechanical condition. Advertisements from the big automakers rarely help because each gives glowing reports about its superior cars and decries the faults of the competition.

When the time comes to evaluate and purchase a car, I rely on the advice of my friends and take a test drive to see how the new vehicle feels.

It would be nice if we could do something similar when we must buy into a system of counseling, but it is even harder to evaluate the different Christian approaches. Books and magazine articles, both secular and Christian, criticize the various methods of counseling and sometimes propose alternatives that aren't very helpful.

"I may sound completely out in left field, but I know I'm right," wrote one highly influential Christian leader:

There would be no need for marriage counseling if husbands and wives would live for God, if they would walk in paths of righteousness, and if they would attempt to abide by the Word of God and pray their problems through. However, we all know that sometimes one or both parties *will not do this*. If they won't, a counseling session won't change anything! An old-fashioned *revival* will change the situation if the Spirit of God is allowed to work in the hearts and lives of the individuals.[1]

No sincere Christian would deny that God works in lives and that he can and often does bring radical change in people who "live for God" and "walk the paths of righteousness." But not even Jesus limited his ministry to revivals. Often he talked to individuals in ways that now would be considered counseling.

His followers today can draw on several Christian therapies that have been carefully developed and are widely used.[2] Are any (or all) of these approaches more effective than the secular theories that some Christians so freely criticize?

Before looking for an answer to this important question, we should consider briefly how counseling is evaluated. Within recent years, secular theorists have tended to move away from personal testimonies about the effectiveness of their psychotherapies and have attempted instead to test their theories scientifically. Christians have applauded this move. If we depend only on subjective statements from individuals or their counselors and ignore careful research, we can prove just about anything we want.[3] Empirical studies and other research investigations are less biased and more accurate indicators of a therapy's degree of effectiveness. When secular therapy does not stand up well to such testing, Christians are often among those who loudly point this out.

In a remarkable example of inconsistency, however, some authors who insist that secular approaches be tested empirically nevertheless propose alternative Christian approaches to counseling that are supported by testimonials only and are not backed by one piece of scientific evidence. One recent Christian book makes the valid criticism that some secular therapists are "long on promises, but short on independent scientific research." These systems are based on the therapists' "own say-so and not upon independent research and followup."[4]

The Christian authors of this book apparently fail to see that the same criticism applies to their own approach to counseling. Because they are built on biblical teachings, Christian approaches rarely get tested but are assumed to be right—even when they disagree with other biblically based methods of counseling.

It is sobering to remind ourselves that terrible heresies have been developed by people who believed the Bible and wanted to live by its principles. Counseling approaches based on the Bible but designed by fallible human beings—including Christians—are not necessarily valid. Even when the counselor has a high view of Scripture and can present a host of testimonials, it does not follow that the lauded approach is consistently effective. If we Christians demand research support from secular therapists and refuse to accept their testimonials, can we demand anything less of ourselves?

Where is the research evidence in support of Christian counseling? There isn't very much, and what we have isn't very encouraging.

Everett L. Worthington, Jr., is a Christian counselor and psychology professor who published a detailed summary of research on "religious counseling."[5] Most likely much of this counseling was done by religious people who did not differ much from secular counselors. But the limited research dealing with conservative evangelical counselors found that they were, in general, *less* effective than counselors who are theologically liberal.

According to Dr. Worthington's study:

1. Most religious counseling is done by clergy. There is evidence that they are not very good counselors, do not feel that they are good counselors and do not get good counselor training in seminaries.

2. Research on religious counseling has focused primarily on pastors or pastoral counselors. Most research has consisted of surveys; almost

no research has studied actual counseling. There are no reported research studies of professionals who openly identify themselves as Christians and neither is there research showing whether Christian marriage counseling is effective.

3. "No support has been found that religious counseling has any more beneficial effects than does secular counseling in working with religious clients. In fact, little is known about what really makes religious counseling distinct from secular counseling, although theory abounds. Anecdotal accounts, theoretical writings, uncontrolled studies and studies of preferences of religious clients suggest that religious clients may benefit from religious counseling, but no outcome research demonstrates this conclusively. The only good studies show secular and religious counseling to be equally effective with religious clients."[6]

Should such findings leave us discouraged about the effectiveness of Christian counseling?

Not necessarily.

Most of us agree with the many writers who proclaim the effectiveness of Christian counseling. In our own lives we have experienced the peace and direction that come with a commitment to Jesus Christ. In counseling, we frequently sense the Holy Spirit's leading in difficult and sensitive situations. Many of us who are believers could give moving testimonials in support of the effectiveness and superiority of Christian counseling.

But if we are to be consistent and fair, we must test our approaches carefully and with the same rigor that we demand of the psychotherapists whose theories we so quickly criticize. If we chide them for relying on testimonials and ignoring research, we must not fall into the same trap. At present, secular writers can criticize Christian counselors by relying on the same arguments that Christians have used to condemn psychotherapy.

For many people, Christian counseling does work. I believe it has helped to bring lasting life changes.

But thus far, this is a conclusion that many have proclaimed but nobody has proven.

Why Are There So Many Different Approaches to Christian Counseling?

11

*P*SYCHOLOGIST HANS H. STRUPP ONCE WROTE A PICTURESQUE DESCRIPTION OF the newcomer's first impression of modern counseling. There is "a welter of theories and practices that seemingly have little in common," Strupp wrote. The casual observer sees

> a melange of practitioners whose philosophical leanings, training, and activities are grossly divergent; a wide range of persons who seek therapy for reasons that are often not very clear; an assortment of human unhappiness, malfunctions, and difficulties that are said to benefit from psychotherapy; a cacophony of claims and counter-claims that therapy is either highly effective or useless; a mixture of awe, fear, and puzzlement that greets the disclosure that someone is "in therapy." Perusal of the *New Yorker* or other magazines shows that therapists are a favorite target for jokes and caricatures.[1]

This description raises the image of different people taking different problems to different therapists who counsel in different ways and get different results. Perhaps you have heard of the medical historian who concluded that "whenever many different remedies are used for a disease, it usually means that we know little about treating the disease."[2] Whenever there are different approaches to counseling, does it also mean that we know little about how to help people with their problems?

If this diversity were characteristic solely of secular psychotherapy, we might argue that differing treatment approaches are inevitable because nonbelievers don't build their systems on the firm foundation of Scripture. But there is also diversity among Christian counselors who take Scripture seriously.

Some Christians who strongly criticize secular therapy criticize other Christian counselors with equal vigor. There are differences of opinion and disagreements between Christian counselors, just as there is diversity in the secular field. Dr. Strupp's description of secular therapies probably applies almost as well to Christian approaches to counseling.

Why do Bible-believing counselors differ so often and so strongly in their views of counseling? There may be several reasons.

Personality reasons. Each of us—counselor and noncounselor, Christian and nonbeliever—has a unique personality, a unique set of past experiences, a unique perspective on life. We have different educational backgrounds, different family constellations, different values, different goals and different characteristics. We decorate our homes differently; prefer different types of recreational activities; have different interests, abilities and aptitudes; and have unique hopes and aspirations.

Is it surprising, then, that we worship in different ways even though we read the same Scriptures and believe in the same God? Don't we have different views about baptism, speaking in tongues or the millennium, even though we all serve the same Christ and seek to obey the same Bible teaching? Is it wrong or evidence of incompetence if students in the same school learn in somewhat different ways, if teachers with similar training use different teaching methods, if licensed medical doctors in the same hospital treat patients in different ways or if equally competent counselors approach their work using different methods?

God doesn't expect believers to be all the same even though they build their worship and service on the same Bible. Within the body of Christ, there are people with different spiritual gifts, unique responsibilities and different degrees of prominence. All are necessary. There is strength in this diversity. It is just what God wants.[3]

Hermeneutical reasons. Hermeneutics is a theological word that refers to "the science and art of biblical interpretation."[4] We don't have to be theologians to realize that people interpret the Bible differently. Sometimes these differences arise because readers make errors in their attempts to understand Scripture.

It is a basic principle of hermeneutics, for example, that phrases, verses and other portions of Scripture should be read in context. If we pull verses and phrases out of the setting in which they appear, we often fall into error or reach conclusions that disagree with those of some other Bible reader.

O. Hobart Mowrer, for example, was a psychologist who appears to have made this mistake. Writing about group counseling, he sometimes quoted James 5:16 to support his position that mutual confession is therapeutic. That verse *does* say, "Confess your sins to each other," but Mowrer's secular perspective led him to ignore its context. If you read the passage you will notice that it speaks mainly about prayer and healing for the physically sick. Mowrer overlooked that. Instead, he suggested that confession of sins to other people is all we need for psychological healing.

Is any one of you in trouble? He should pray. Is anyone happy? Let him sing songs of praise. Is any one of you sick? He should call the elders of the church to pray over him and anoint him with oil in the name of the Lord. And the prayer offered in faith will make the sick person well; the Lord will raise him up. If he has sinned, he will be forgiven. Therefore confess your sins to each other and pray for each other so that you may be healed. The prayer of a righteous man is powerful and effective. (Jas 5:13-16)

It is another principle of hermeneutics that Bible readers should read the whole of Scripture, not just the parts with which they agree. Some Christian counselors emphasize love but overlook biblical teachings on sin and repentance. Others emphasize the importance of confrontation in counseling but say little about the even greater biblical emphasis on encouragement and building people up.

This tendency to see what we want to see and to overlook what we prefer to ignore is called "selective hermeneutics." It is an error into which even the most careful Bible readers sometimes fall.

A third principle of hermeneutics says that we should base our conclusions on the clear passages of Scripture rather than on obscure or difficult-to-understand Bible verses. Some of the world's greatest heresies come because readers overlook clear biblical teaching. Instead, they create fanciful systems that have debatable validity because they are built on obscure Bible passages.

I encourage all my Christian counseling students to take a basic course in hermeneutics. It is an important part of their training. It helps in their personal Bible study and it also enables them more clearly to evaluate Christian counseling theories that claim to be built on a biblical foundation but propose differing approaches to people-helping.[5]

Theological reasons. Students who study counseling theories often discover that they are attracted to certain positions and inclined to reject others. This personal preference appears to be more related to the student's personality than to the evidence in support of any one theory.

Is it also possible that we prefer approaches that best fit with our theological views? Many Christians have been impressed with Glasser's Reality Therapy because of its emphasis on loving involvement and responsibility.[6] Others like the Calvinistic emphasis apparent in the writings of Jay Adams,[7] or the "Keswick theology" in Charles R. Solomon's spirituotherapy.[8] It should come as no surprise that different theological positions give rise to different approaches to Christian counseling.[9]

Research evidence has shown impressively that there is no difference in effectiveness between the various secular approaches to psychotherapy. They all work about equally well.[10] Could the same be said for the

Christian approaches? There is no research evidence to show that some Christian counselors are more effective than others. According to one report, the research to date shows no evidence that "religious counseling has any more beneficial effects than does secular counseling in working with religious clients."[11]

It is sad, therefore, to hear about a church that splits down the middle over the issue of which approach to counseling is best. Debate about counseling methods and theories can be intellectually challenging and ultimately helpful to counselees. But when we argue without listening, or when we display a superior "my-way-is-the-only-biblical-way" attitude that shows no appreciation for other Christian approaches, then are we much different from the secular psychotherapists we so often criticize? And does the debate do anything to honor Christ or help counselees get better?

Why Would a Christian Counselor Use Secular Counseling Methods?

12

I COULDN'T TELL WHETHER THE LETTER SHOWED ANGER, DISAPPOINTMENT OR both. It came from a Christian psychologist who had written to complain about one of my former students.

"I am glad that he is a committed believer," the letter stated, "but this counselor bases his methods on secular humanism. He seems more interested in using secular methods than biblical methods to help people."

In responding to the letter, I made no attempt to defend the former student. He had chosen his own methods of counseling and apparently had accepted completely secular theoretical viewpoints.

In his survey of religious counseling, psychologist Everett Worthington found that Christians have three views about counseling techniques.[1] First, some like my former student believe that religious counseling involves using established secular methods to help counselees with their religious concerns and problems. Critics of this view, like the man who wrote that letter, argue that if only secular techniques and theories are used, then the counseling is secular. It is not religious, and it certainly isn't Christian, despite the counselor's personal beliefs.

A second view states that religious counseling must draw all its techniques from theology or religion. Advocates of this view believe "it is possible to minister to mental-emotional-behavioral problems without resorting to psychological models or to psychological gimmicks and devices."[2] Spiritual guidance, prayer, confession of sin, meditation on Scripture, involvement in a caring church and similar biblical concepts are seen as the only ways to help hurting people. Critics argue that these methods promote religious education, discipleship or spiritual growth, but they aren't counseling techniques.

The issue becomes even more complicated when we add a third viewpoint that attempts to combine the first two. Secular theories and approaches are combined with religious methods in an effort to help people with their problems, values and personal struggles. Critics of this view proclaim loudly that such integration of the secular with the biblical is impossible.

Is it?[3]

One guidebook suggests that psychological counseling provides manmade, nonscientific solutions to mental-emotional-behavioral problems.[4] In contrast, biblical counseling "is not based on the theories or techniques of men, but rather is practiced by those who know the Bible, have applied God's Word in their own lives by the enabling power of · the Holy Spirit, and love others in such as way as to minister healing and life."[5] In practicing this form of counseling, however, it surely is not possible to avoid all techniques that appear to be manmade or used by secular therapists.

Psychological counseling and spiritual counseling *both* involve "listening and learning, gaining understanding into thought and behavior, and discovering and implementing changes."[6] Both may involve teaching, correcting, training, accepting, building up, advising, showing patience, comforting, strengthening, giving hope and being objective without losing compassion.[7] Both may encourage verbal confession, changes in thinking and emotion, behavioral change, involvement with support groups, diary keeping, physical exercise, involvement in artistic expression, or discussion of the past week's activities.[8] None of these is uniquely biblical; none is solely psychological.

It would be unrealistic to imply that Christian counseling methods never overlap with those of secular psychologists. It is inconsistent to criticize all psychological methods because they are "secular and manmade" but then use many of these same methods, proclaiming that they are uniquely biblical. Christian counselors can and do use a variety of techniques that are part of both secular and biblical counseling.

Regrettably, however, some Christian counselors (including, I suspect, that former student) give little thought to the uniqueness of biblical counseling and do nothing different from secular counselors who build on humanistic presuppositions.

True Christian counseling involves more than secular counseling. Christian counseling points people to the teachings of Scripture and encourages counselees to live in accordance with the Word of God. This is not done in an insensitive way that ignores the counselee's values, condemns his or her beliefs before any kind of rapport has been built, or applies some kind of memorized counseling formula.

Instead, we must be like Paul, who understood the people at Athens, listened to their struggles and debates, respected them as individuals in spite of their theological ignorance, and won the right to be heard before he presented the truth of the gospel (Acts 17:16-34). When Paul preached and counseled, he presumably used persuasion and debating techniques that were neither completely secular nor solely Christian. In all his ministry, he was careful never to use any method that would suggest non-Christian values or be inconsistent with scriptural teaching. But the real uniqueness of Paul's approach was in the content of his message, not in the techniques he used to present it.

The same is true of counseling. Like their secular colleagues, Christian counselors at times may make suggestions, help with goal-setting, give guidance or use a variety of other similar methods. But none of this counseling is value-free. Both the Christian and the nonbeliever have values that influence counseling. The follower of Christ cannot encourage counselees to make decisions or engage in behavior that is not in accord with biblical teaching.

The Christian counselor seeks to be used by God to touch and change each counselee's life. The counselor freely admits his or her Christian values and commitment, prays for counselees consistently, trusts God to bring healing and give wisdom, encourages behavior and thinking that is consistent with scriptural truth, and sensitively shares what God's Word says about morality, marriage, sin, forgiveness, interpersonal relationships, bitterness, anxiety and similar issues. Where the Bible is silent on an issue, the Christian asks for the Holy Spirit's special guidance and seeks to counsel in ways that are consistent with the general principles of Scripture.

As a believer, the Christian counselor's personal life should reflect an attitude of submission to God, an awareness of the influence and deceptive practices of Satan, an active involvement in some local body of believers, and a consistent personal devotional life of prayer, meditation and Bible reading.

When such a person does counseling, he or she may use techniques that some consider secular—just as the Christian physician uses "secular" medical techniques, the Christian banker uses "secular" banking methods, and the Christian legislator uses "secular" approaches to lawmaking. In these and other fields some methods must be rejected because they are clearly immoral and nonbiblical, just as others must be accepted and used because they are biblical and uniquely Christian. But there is also overlap, and often Christian counselors find themselves using methods that others brand "secular." Christian counselors use secular methods when these are helpful, practical, generally consistent with biblical teaching, and used or mentioned approvingly by biblical writers.

I once read a humorous and overstated story about a man who refused to wear gloves, celebrate Christmas or use toothpaste because secular humanists did all of these. We couldn't survive if we avoided everything used by nonbelievers. In the same way, we couldn't counsel if we rejected all helping methods used by non-Christians. Instead, Christian counselors must be sure that their methods—even those that some consider secular—are consistent with and tested against the divine Word of God.

Can Christian Counselors Help Non-Christians?

*T*HE MAN DIDN'T AGREE WITH MY APPROACH TO COUNSELING.

That was apparent even before he rose from his seat during the discussion period following my lecture.

"I start all my counseling sessions in the same way," he began. "I tell the person who comes for help that I don't even want to hear about the problem until we deal with a basic spiritual question: Have you been born again? If the counselee is a believer, we go on to the problem. If not, I present the gospel and state that I can't help people unless and until they have committed themselves to Jesus Christ."

I admired the man's evangelistic zeal, but I wondered how many people had been turned away by his insensitive and rigid approach. Bringing people to Christ is the essence of the Great Commission (Mt 28:19-20), but from this it does not follow that Christian counselors should offer help only to believers.

It is always easiest to counsel with people who share our beliefs. When they have similar values, counselors and their clients are more inclined to like each other, the counselees are more trusting, there is more likely to be counselee growth, and the counseling will be more successful.[1]

Even when they come from different denominational backgrounds, Christians tend to share language, perspectives, beliefs, hopes, attitudes, scriptural promises and standards of right and wrong. In most situations, counseling is easier when the counselor and counselee are both believers. In some respects, therefore, it is easy to understand that man who refused to counsel nonbelievers and determined to "get each person saved" before counseling could begin.

Still, there are reasons to question his approach.

Jesus helped nonbelievers. Jesus spent time with sinners, healed a Roman centurion's slave, counseled a hated tax collector, drove demons out of a heathen pig rancher, and freely taught anyone who would listen. Jesus was willing to reach out and help nonbelievers. Shouldn't his followers do the same?

The Scriptures do not instruct us to limit our helping to believers. In writing to the Galatians, Paul instructed believers to gently restore anyone who had fallen into sin. He emphasized mutual burden bearing, counselor humility and the importance of personal responsibility (Gal 6:1-8). Then the apostle wrote: "Let us not become weary in doing good, for at the proper time we will reap a harvest if we do not give up. Therefore, as we have opportunity, let us do good to all people, especially to those who belong to the family of believers" (Gal 6:9-10).

We who are part of that family of believers must follow the example of Jesus, who "went around doing good" (Acts 10:38). We may work most effectively with fellow Christians, but this does not excuse us from giving help, including counseling help, to "all people" who might be in need.

Most experienced Christian counselors do not limit their helping to believers. I suspect that most Christian counselors would disagree with the man who spoke following my lecture. Sometimes counseling with nonbelievers is a good way to build rapport so that counselees are more open to hearing the gospel later. We already know that when counseling is effective, counselees tend to change their values and become more like their counselors.[2] Good counseling, therefore, could be a form of pre-evangelism.

Even strong advocates of evangelism warn against an insensitive and ill-timed sharing of the gospel with counselees. I agree with Jay Adams's position that any counseling that claims to be Christian must surely be evangelistic. But "counselors must be careful not to represent Christ as the member of a first-aid squad who offers bandaids to clients."[3] This appeared to be the approach of the man in my lecture meeting. Committed to evangelism, he was intent on dispensing the gospel as a first-aid treatment even before listening to the counselee's problems or earning the right to be heard.

None of this excuses the Christian counselor from sharing the gospel with nonbelievers. No sensitive counselor wants to take advantage of hurting clients or to push religious views on people who have come requesting some other kind of help. It is professionally unethical to force religion on counselees, and surely it is not consistent with biblical teaching to manipulate people so they are forced to make decisions about Christianity.

Too often, however, Christian counselors say nothing about the gospel. Counselees can come for an entire series of counseling sessions and never know the counselor is a believer. Critics of psychology correctly argue that Christians are failing their counselees if discussion focuses exclusively on secular methods and humanistic theories. Counseling can hardly be called Christian if counselees are helped to solve problems or cope with stress but are never made aware of their sin or told of their need for the Savior.

Do we believe that Jesus Christ can change lives? Are we convinced that people will find ultimate forgiveness, joy, inner peace, security and healing only when they know Christ? Do we believe that the Bible, God's Word, has insights about love, morals, standards of living, human destiny, and similar issues that psychology alone cannot understand? Are we counselors willing to let the Holy Spirit give us understanding in our thoughts and words, and wisdom in our counseling procedures? If the answer to these questions is no, then we have accepted a theology that surely is not what the Bible teaches. If we answer yes, is there any justification for keeping this information to ourselves?

Certainly the counselor respects his or her clients and does not push religion. Like a doctor with a new cure, however, a Christian counselor is ethically bound to make the healing balm of scriptural truth available to hurting counselees who could profit from biblical treatment sensitively and lovingly applied, whenever and however the Holy Spirit leads.

Should the gospel be presented automatically, as soon as the counselee walks through the door? *No.*

Should nonbelievers hear the gospel and be introduced to biblical principles as part of their counseling? In my opinion, the answer is a clear *Yes.*

This certainly will not happen, however, if Christian counselors refuse to help nonbelievers.

Should a Christian Bother to Get Counselor Training?

14

CHRISTY IS A JUNIOR HIGH-SCHOOL STUDENT WHO CALLED ABOUT A CLASS assignment. "We're supposed to choose some vocation that interests us," she said. "Then the teacher wants us to find and interview somebody who is in that type of work."

Christy wants to be a psychologist, and when she heard about me, she asked me to be the subject of her interview.

All was going well until Christy asked about training for psychologists. I could tell she was surprised when we went over the requirements: finish junior high and high school, get a college degree, go on to graduate school for a doctor's degree, and take at least a year of internship. Then, if she passes her licensing exam, the state will certify her as a professional counselor.

Psychiatrists, social workers and other professional groups have different requirements, but most involve a lengthy training period. Christy wondered if this all was necessary.

Many would say it is not. E. Fuller Torrey is a psychiatrist who believes that most professional counselors work not with people who are mentally ill, but with those who have "problems of living."[1] These problems are rarely discussed in professional training programs. Instead, the emphasis is on theories, methods and pathologies far removed from the issues most people bring to counselors. Psychoanalysts argue that many years of arduous, expensive, in-depth training is needed if one is to be a competent therapist, but recent evidence suggests that neither long-term training nor long-term treatment is needed in order to help hurting people.[2] One survey of research has produced a powerful conclusion: "Professional mental health education, training, and experience do not appear to be necessary prerequisites for an effective helping person."[3]

How, then, do we respond to Christy's question, "Do you really have to get all this training if you want to counsel?"

Our answer is both yes and no. The requirements differ from place to place, but most states will issue a license to counsel professionally only after a certain level of academic training has been successfully completed. It may be true that much of the training is irrelevant, but it is a legal prerequisite to calling oneself a psychiatrist or psychologist, charging fees or opening a private practice.

Not everyone chooses to be in private practice, however. To counsel in a school, college, business or other place where one is paid, the requirements are less demanding. To counsel in a church, there are few requirements at all. Most pastoral counselors have only a course or two in counseling. The members of the congregation, even with no training, may counsel their friends if they want to, so long as they don't charge money or call themselves psychologists. Christy can start counseling now with her friends at the junior high.

Let us assume, however, that she wants to pursue a career in counseling. Does it make sense for Christy or anybody else to spend time, energy and money to get professional training? Since Christy is a Christian, is it good stewardship for her to devote some of the best years of her life to the academic study of psychology and counseling?

If Christy wants to be a professional counselor with a private practice, she will have no alternative to a long period of training. She may be encouraged to know that there are now several masters and doctoral-level training programs that have a clear Christian emphasis, that focus on biblical methods of counseling and that prepare counselors to meet professional training standards.

If she enrolls in a good training program, Christy will learn about the traditional theories and methods of therapy, but she will also learn how to do and evaluate the kind of scientific research that lets us know which counseling methods are most effective. Christy will read and critique the writings of those who criticize psychotherapy as well as the works of those who proclaim counseling's effectiveness.

If her training is good, Christy will discover that much of her learning takes place away from the library. Developing listening skills, learning how to be sensitive, practicing appropriate responses, observing the work of master counselor-teachers, listening to tapes of effective counseling and actually doing counseling under careful supervision will all be part of the training program. Christy will find that we don't learn to be effective counselors if we spend all our time reading books, writing papers or preparing a scholarly thesis.

As a Christian, Christy will quickly discover that psychological insights and techniques can be valuable, but by themselves they are of limited effectiveness. She will need to read, study and understand the Scriptures, to be involved with a local church and to discipline herself to spend regular periods of time in prayer. If she is to be competent as a counselor, she will ask daily for the Holy Spirit's guidance, sensitivity, understanding, strength, power and wisdom to direct as she meets with her counselees. She will recognize that Christian counselors, like all believers, are involved in spiritual battles that cannot be fought in human strength (Eph 6:10-18). She will pray for spiritual protection to keep her from falling into sin and to keep her thinking pure even as she listens to tales of immorality.

Christy will undoubtedly hear criticisms of her training—probably every profession criticizes its educational programs. In my twenty years of teaching in theological schools, I have heard repeatedly that seminary training really doesn't prepare young men and women for the ministry. Does a Master's degree in Business Administration (MBA) really prepare one for business? Are registered nurses effectively prepared by their educational experiences? Do programs in elementary or secondary education competently train teachers?

Along with their strengths, most training programs have weaknesses. This is surely true of counselor training. There must be constant efforts to improve and evaluate the training programs intended to teach people how to counsel.

Even as counselor education improves, not all students will benefit from their training. Some study counseling for months or years, acquiring impressive knowledge about counseling, but they are insensitive and ineffective as practical people-helpers. In contrast, others seem to be effective counselors even though they have never read a counseling book or heard about theories of psychotherapy. How do we explain this difference?

According to the Bible, all believers are expected to help and show practical concern for others. We are instructed to "do good to all" people, especially fellow Christians (Gal 6:10).[4] When others have needs, those motivated by Christian love will be involved in counseling whether or not they have training.

Is it possible, however, that some Christians are especially gifted as counselors? "That counseling is one of the eighteen or so 'spiritual gifts' is not to me a debatable matter," wrote psychologist Paul Morris. Nevertheless,

> God has not given every believer this gift any more than he has given each believer the gift of "tongues" or of "pastor-teacher."
>
> I know people who have never been to seminary and yet possess this gift. I wouldn't be afraid to trust these people with my mother or even the worst "incurable" psychotic. These are the most competent counselors in the world. . . . These men and women have been

given *supernatural ability* by God, which they did not possess before he gave it.[5]

The gift of exhortation is mentioned in Romans 12:8. The Greek work is *paraklesis,* which means "coming alongside to help." The word implies activities such as encouraging, supporting, admonishing and comforting. All this sounds like counseling—the kind of counseling that was done by Jesus. Many would agree that it is a gift given by God to a select group of believers.

Even gifted people can benefit from training and experience, but it doesn't take long to discover that no teacher is perfect, no psychological theory always works, and no biblical interpretation is infallible. Even so, we can and do learn from others. This includes learning to counsel more effectively.

I doubt if she wants to hear this, but if Christy wants to be a professionally qualified counselor, she'll have to spend a lot more time in school. Even so, there is no solid evidence to guarantee that this training will make her a better counselor.

Is Mental Health the Same as Christian Maturity?

I WASN'T AT THE MEETING, BUT I HEARD ABOUT IT.

Several years ago a respected Christian psychologist gave a major speech in which he argued that the fruit of the Spirit—love, joy, peace, patience, kindness, goodness, faithfulness, gentleness and self-control (Gal 5:22)—could all be produced by psychological techniques alone. There was no need to wait for the Holy Spirit to develop these, the speaker maintained. They could all be duplicated by any competent psychologist.

The audience reaction was predictable. Many expressed shock and strong disagreement. Some called the speech heresy. The speaker replied that, in his opinion, spiritual maturity and psychological health are really the same thing. They can be produced either psychologically or spiritually.

Is this a valid conclusion? The question is not easily answered; there are no clear, universally accepted definitions of either mental health or Christian maturity.[1]

What is mental health? Many years ago an educator, a statistician, a sociologist, an anthropologist, a philosopher, a lawyer, a psychoanalyst, a botanist, a psychiatrist, a neurologist, a theologian and a psychologist met together to discuss what is meant by "normal behavior." Each defined *normal* and *abnormal* in slightly different ways, and the experts were unable to agree on definitions acceptable to everyone.[2]

A similar problem faces those who want to define *mental health*.

Some say that mental health is the absence of psychological abnormality. According to one Christian perspective, people are abnormal, and thus not mentally healthy, if their behavior is at odds with the society in which they live; if they experience internal conflicts that lead to intense and prolonged feelings of insecurity, anxiety or unhappiness; and if they are alienated or away from God.[3] This suggests that in order to be mentally healthy, one would have to be at peace with one's society, at peace with oneself and at peace with God.

More often, mental health is described, not as the absence of abnormality, but in terms of positive personal characteristics. It has been suggested, for example, that to be mentally healthy one must have—

☐ a realistic and accurate view of oneself and others

☐ an accurate perception of the environment

☐ the willingness to accept one's own strengths and weaknesses

☐ the ability to live in the present but have long-range goals

☐ a system of values including clear standards of right and wrong

☐ a feeling of independence and autonomy along with the realization that we all need other people

☐ the ability to cope with problems and accept responsibilities

☐ the ability to give love and to treat others with respect

☐ the acceptance of feelings and the ability to control emotion

☐ the development of one's capabilities, interests and skills for living[4]

According to this description, nonbelievers and Christians both can and often do reach a state of mental health.

What is Christian maturity? Most of us would agree that Jesus, more than any other, met the standards of mental health listed above. But Jesus had something extra. He was intent on doing the will of his Father. His life reflected the fruit of the Spirit. He was holy, resistant to sinful temptations, led by the Holy Spirit, compassionate, intent on doing good, intimately acquainted with the Scriptures, devoted to prayer and self-disciplined. In short, he was like his Father in heaven.

The Christian, even the maturing and growing Christian, falls far short of this standard. But the believer's goal is to be perfect, even as the heavenly Father is perfect (Mt 5:48). Each of us is to be like Jesus. We are to train ourselves to be godly (1 Tim 4:7), and, as God's chosen people, we are to "clothe ourselves" with compassion, kindness, humility, gentleness and patience (Col 3:12).

Most Christians believe that goals such as these cannot be reached in human strength alone. Christian growth comes only to those who first have been born again (Jn 3:3-18) by confessing their sins and believing that Jesus, God's Son, alone is able to forgive sin and give eternal life. Christians believe that the Holy Spirit lives within our lives and gives the strength and wisdom to grow in Christlikeness. The psychologist may attempt to duplicate the characteristics (or fruit) of the Spirit, but only the Holy Spirit himself enables believers to grow in the love, joy, peace and other spiritual traits the Bible describes (Gal 5:22-23).

Christian maturity, then, is similar to mental health, but the two are not identical.

Do Christian maturity and mental health always go together?

Not necessarily.

Many churches are filled with squabbling, backbiting, self-centered, immature, narrow-minded people. I wish we could argue that this isn't so, but Christian growth is slow, and many remain "babes in Christ" (1 Cor 3:1-3) their entire lives. Such people often are caught up in jealousy, magical thinking, self-justification and the pursuit of their own comforts.[5] They are believers who have the potential for Christian growth, but they are neither spiritually mature nor mentally healthy.

All this leads to the conclusion that—
☐ Some people are neither mentally healthy nor maturing spiritually.
☐ Some people are both mentally healthy and maturing spiritually.
☐ Some people are mentally healthy but are not maturing spiritually.
Is it possible to be spiritually maturing but not mentally healthy?

Look again at our description of mental health. It may be possible for believers to mature spiritually and remain psychologically unhealthy, but this seems rare and unlikely. If the believer's goal is to be like Jesus, he or she will be characterized by both psychological and spiritual growth.

Again we must emphasize that all persons fall short of these ideals. In spiritual growth and psychological maturity each believer should be in the process of what psychologist Gordon Allport has called "becoming."[6] Guided by the Holy Spirit, committed Christians are becoming more Christlike and spiritually mature. At the same time, all of us can have the goal of becoming more healthy mentally.

Christian maturity and mental health go together often—but not always.

PART THREE
Questions about How Christianity and Psychology Conflict

Jesus and Paul Never Used Psychology— So Why Should We?

16

*I*F JESUS OR PAUL RETURNED TO THE EARTH TODAY, DO YOU THINK EITHER ONE would ever enroll in a psychology course or read a psychology textbook?

Jesus was the perfect, wonderful counselor centuries before anyone had heard of psychiatry or clinical psychology. He had all the knowledge and wisdom he needed to counsel effectively.[1] If psychology had been taught at the universities when he walked on the earth, Jesus probably would not have taken the course because he didn't have to. His knowledge of human behavior was infinite and perfect.

Paul, in contrast, did not have Jesus' infinite understanding, but he was a well-educated intellectual who understood many of the world's philosophies. He rejected the notion that these could give ultimate answers to human questions. Instead he built many of his arguments on Scripture and insisted that the scholars of his time repent. Surely the apostle would have presented a similar message to psychological scholars if they had existed when Paul was alive.

Does it follow, however, that the modern disciple of Christ and reader of Paul's epistles should throw away psychology books and reject psychology because it was not used centuries ago?

To begin our answer, let us recognize that some modern developments *are* acceptable to almost all Christians, even though they never were used in the early church. Jesus and Paul never spoke on the radio, never used a microphone, never took antibiotics, never used a computer, never had a tooth filled painlessly, never ate ice cream or rode in a car—but nobody says these are wrong because first-century people knew nothing about them. Clearly there are some modern conveniences, ideas and technological advances that are fine for our use even though Jesus and Paul never used them.

But psychology, say the critics, is not in the same category as microphones, antibiotics or ice cream cones. Psychology deals with the very issues discussed in the Bible. "For almost two-thousand years the church did without the pseudoscience of psychotherapy and still was able to minister successfully to those burdened by the problems of living."[2] Why, then, should we bother with psychology today?

Psychology, as we have seen, is diverse, and even its critics acknowledge that some parts need not be rejected. "Psychology may have some value in helping us understand man's predicament from a different perspective," writes a pastor in an article generally critical of psychologists.[3] Another writes that we can "leave the door open for help . . . from qualified psychologists who deal with such things as learning problems and the probable conduct of a psychotic or alcoholic husband or wife."[4] "We are not opposed to, nor are we criticizing, the entire field of psychology," states another book.[5] These authors instead are distressed with those parts of psychology that propose to help people using ideologies that appear to contradict Scripture.

I agree that ideologies—psychological or otherwise—must not be accepted or used if they contradict the Bible. Committed believers must not try to merge antibiblical psychologies with the clear truths of Scripture. Counseling methods that advocate immoral behavior, for example, can never be used by Christian people-helpers. Most would agree that even well-meaning and sincere Christian psychologists can be contaminated by the secular assumptions and practices that pervade much of modern psychology.[6]

From this it does not follow, however, that all counseling methods are antibiblical or that psychology has nothing of value to contribute to helping and understanding people.

Could it be, instead, that psychology is a God-given field of knowledge? Might it be an academic and practical discipline enabling us more adequately to help people who live in a society permeated with change and complexity unknown in the days of Jesus and Paul?

Nobody, and certainly no committed believer, suggests that psychology is without error. The Bible is the only book without error. Even theology and man-created systems of "Christian counseling" are the work of fallible, error-prone, sin-influenced human beings. Psychological conclusions, psychotherapeutic practices, counseling principles, psychiatric theories—all these, like every other area of study, must be examined carefully under the probing light of Scripture.

The Bible deals with preaching, but we don't reject all modern homiletics and principles of public speaking because these were unknown in ancient Jerusalem. Jesus and Paul both taught and wrote about teaching, but we don't dismiss modern methods of education, including Christian education, because these were not known in Bible times. The Scriptures are filled with references to healing, but we don't cast aside all contemporary forms of medicine because they were not used in the early Christian church. Surely there is much modern knowledge that was unknown in the days of Jesus and Paul but has been given by God to help us minister to one another and serve Christ more effectively.

Consider, for example, modern principles of stress management. Perhaps there was little need for these prior to our current pressure-filled age. So long as they do not contradict or even suggest a disagreement with the Bible, can we not use these modern coping methods and receive them with thanks? Why not acknowledge that God may have made them available for our use in times such as these?

It is not valid, scholarly or wise to admit that progress is possible in almost every area of knowledge except clinical and counseling psychology. If Jesus or Paul returned to earth today, they might rejoice in the advances of modern technology that make wide-scale evangelism possible. Surely they would not seal the advances of secular counseling in a little box labeled "Contaminated and harmful—Do not touch."

I doubt that Jesus or Paul would be likely to throw away psychology—as some contemporary Christians might hope. As a formal discipline, psychology was not available in Bible times; but it is available now and can be used by believers, with thanksgiving.

What Good Is Psychology If the Bible Tells Us All We Need to Know?

17

I WONDER HOW MANY TIMES I'VE SEEN IT.

You've probably seen it too.

In the midst of a sermon the preacher holds the Bible high in the air and proclaims enthusiastically, "This book has all the answers to all our problems!"

And some of the people say, "Amen!"

A similar message has appeared in some Christian books about psychology. There is "no unique problem that has not been mentioned plainly in the Scriptures," writes one author. There is "a biblical solution to every problem."[1]

"We maintain that God and His Word provide a completely sufficient foundation for mental-emotional health and that the Bible is the repository of the healing balm for *all* nonorganically based mental-emotional disorders," writes another.[2]

More recently, a respected pastor published a similar conclusion:

Peter writes that our Lord's divine power has granted us "everything pertaining to life and godliness, through the true knowledge of Him who called us by His own glory and excellence" (2 Peter 1:3).

Paul writes, "For in Him all the fullness of deity dwells in bodily form, and in Him you have been made complete, and He is the head over all rule and authority" (Col. 2:9, 10). This leaves little room for using the techniques of secular psychology to help Christians achieve emotional and spiritual wholeness.[3]

To challenge such statements is to risk being misunderstood and criticized. But do some some sincere preachers claim more for the Bible than it claims for itself?

The Bible is the inspired, valid, true Word of God.[4] Let us begin with this basic belief. It was written by godly people who were guided by the Holy Spirit as they wrote (2 Pet 1:21). It is an intensely practical book that "is useful to teach us what is true and to make us realize what is wrong in our lives; it straightens us out and helps us do what is right. It is God's way of making us well prepared at every point, fully equipped to do good to everyone" (2 Tim 3:16-17 LB).

Even though the Bible is all true, it does not follow that all truth is in the Bible. Most biblical scholars would accept this statement. In mathematics, medicine, physics, geography, marine biology and a host of other areas, there is much truth that is not mentioned in the Bible. God in his wisdom has allowed human beings to discover truths about the universe that are not discussed in Scripture.

Some critics of psychology seem to argue, however, that God has not allowed human beings to discover any truths about interpersonal relations, mental health, counseling techniques, mental disorders, personal decision making or any other issues related to stress management and daily living. Such a view maintains that God has allowed human beings to discover truth in almost every field of human study except psychology.

All truths discovered by human beings must be tested against and proved consistent with the revealed Word of God. If the Bible is true, we cannot have psychological discoveries that are also true but inconsistent with the Scriptures. The Christian scholar tests his or her findings against the Scriptures; we do not try to validate the Scriptures by testing them against knowledge discovered by human endeavor. To state this more specifically: the Christian tests psychology against the Bible, not the Bible against psychology.

At times this checking process is not easy. Many scriptural texts are interpreted differently by Bible scholars. In addition, human knowledge and scriptural teachings sometimes deal with such unrelated topics that there is no overlap. Mathematics, medicine, physics, computer technology or marine biology, for example, have no conflict with Scripture because these areas of study are not mentioned in the Bible.

When we discuss principles of living and interpersonal relations, however, we must be much more careful because many—though not all—of these *are* discussed in the Bible. Psychological conclusions or counseling techniques must be rejected if they conflict with clear biblical teachings or with our best interpretations of Scripture.

Some human problems are not mentioned in the Scriptures. They are not discussed specifically, and neither are there examples to show how others dealt with these issues in a way pleasing to God. The Bible was not written as a self-help, question-and-answer book covering every possible human problem. It does not claim to be a textbook of counseling techniques or personal problem solving. Surely we should not force it to be something that it does not claim to be.

Think of the kinds of problems people bring to counselors:

"I've been accepted by two Christian colleges. I can't decide which one to attend."

"Should I get married now, or wait until I am well launched on my career?"

"I know God has forgiven me for my past sins, but what do I do now that I'm pregnant?"

"How can I stop eating so much?"

"I am really depressed. The doctor says there is nothing physically causing this, and I can't think of any sin in my life that might be pulling me down. What should I do?"

"Can you help me? I've got AIDS."

"I keep failing math. How can I get through the course so I can graduate?"

"My father abused me when I was a child. I have asked the Lord to help me forget. I have forgiven my father, but we can't discuss it because he is no longer alive. Still, I can't shake the hurt, and it is adversely affecting my marriage. What do I do?"

"I am anxious all the time. I have asked the Lord to give me peace, but I still panic frequently."

Many, perhaps most, of the problems people bring to modern counselors are never discussed in the Bible.

Often principles of behavior can be inferred from the Bible and applied to modern problems. The Scriptures, for example, say nothing about R-rated movies or about whether Christians should watch television soap operas. But the Bible does tell us to avoid and flee from sexual immorality (1 Thess 4:3; 1 Cor 6:18), to develop pure minds characterized by wholesome thinking (2 Pet 3:1), to live godly, holy lives (2 Pet 3:11), to be self-controlled (1 Pet 1:13) and to have Christlike minds (1 Cor 2:16; Phil 2:5 KJV). These scriptural principles provide good reason to keep our minds free of lustful thinking, to be "wise about what is good, and innocent about what is evil" (Rom 16:19). These Bible verses make a good case for avoiding sexually stimulating and immoral films and television shows.

But do principles like these cover all the personal problems not mentioned specifically in Scripture? It would be difficult to find scriptural principles to guide in all the sample problems we have listed. Surely there are times, many times, when a sensitive, psychologically trained, committed Christian counselor can help people through psychological techniques and with psychological insights that God has allowed us to discover, but that he has not chosen to reveal in the Bible. This does not assume that psychology is replacing Scripture or that the Holy Spirit can no longer bring healing. We assume, instead, that God in his sovereign wisdom works to accomplish his purposes through the training and caring skills of modern believers, just as he has done in the past.

Recently I read a magazine advertisement that began with these words: "Although people have real problems, thankfully the Word of God has the answers." Most of us would agree.

But the Word of God never claims to have *all* the answers to all of life's problems.

The Bible speaks to human needs today. It always will. But God in his goodness also has allowed us to discover psychological truths about human behavior and counseling that are never mentioned in Scripture but are consistent with the written Word of God and helpful to people facing the problems of modern living.

Is Psychology a New Religion That Competes with Christianity?

18

AT THE BEGINNING OF THIS CENTURY, PSYCHOLOGISTS WERE RARE. COLLEGE psychology courses were almost nonexistent. There were only a few psychology texts, and nobody had heard of self-help books.

But all this has changed. By the early 1970s psychology had become the most popular major among college students. Introductory textbooks in psychology rolled off the presses in great numbers. Students clamored to get into graduate schools—as many still do today. Membership in the American Psychological Association is expected to pass 100,000 within a few years. Self-help psychology books, many written from a Christian perspective, now fill bookstore shelves and are among the biggest sellers in the publishing industry.

This fascination with psychology is especially prominent in America. One-third of the world's psychiatrists are Americans, and well over half of all clinical psychologists live in the United States. There are more professional therapists in this country than librarians, firefighters or mail carriers. Professional counselors outnumber dentists and pharmacists by a ratio of almost two to one.[1] At the rate we are going, mused Harvard psychologist E. G. Boring, someday "there will be more psychologists than people in this country."[2]

Why has psychology become so popular? Some have suggested that Freud's thinking was a prime stimulus for this growth. Freud's initial ideas about dream interpretation, the unconscious, sex, slips of the tongue, the ego and other psychoanalytic concepts have long been rejected or modified by mainstream psychology, but even Freud's critics admit that the influence of this quiet Jewish man from Vienna has gone far beyond counseling or the field of psychiatry. Freudian thinking has had a tremendous impact on the thinking, values, direction and psychology of Western society.

Ours is one of very few societies in history where people have enough leisure time to think about their goals, hang-ups, aspirations, lack of fulfillment and ways to find meaning—all topics dealt with by psychology. Many people today have "too much money and not enough to do," writes Jerome Frank, perhaps with tongue in cheek. As a result "they turn to psychotherapy to combat the resulting boredom. It supplies novelty, excitement and, as a means of self-improvement, a legitimate way of spending money. Today hosts of persons seek psychotherapy for discomforts that a less affluent society would regard as trivial."[3]

Perhaps part of psychology's growth has come because of the anxiety in our times. Thanks to the media, we know about wars, rumors of wars, economic depressions, disasters, threats of disasters and personal tragedy almost as soon as they happen. This keeps us informed, but it also creates anxiety. Media advertising presents the good life, but does this also create dissatisfaction and push people to strive for more possessions? Do glamorous dramas, unrealistic cartoons and opulent game shows create dissatisfaction in the lives of those who watch spellbound in their small, underfurnished living rooms? Has all the talk about baby-boomers and competition for success created tension in the lives of career-age people? None of this can be proven conclusively, but it may be that the information explosion of the present age has also created an anxiety explosion, along with a desire for psychological help.

It also is possible that the growth of psychology has come because of the widespread decline in religious interest and activity. This decline in the popularity of religion surely leaves many people without values, meaning or hope. Theological beliefs that have guided people for centuries now are thought to be irrelevant or too simplistic for sophisticated modern thinkers. To replace our fading traditions and long-established sources of authority, Western society has turned to a new source of hope and values: a psychological movement that claims to be scientific and thoroughly up to date. Has a psychological movement that criticizes formal religion itself become a substitute religion?

Is psychology a new religion? Before considering this question, we should remind ourselves that psychology, like psychiatry and other related areas, is a diverse field. There is little popular interest in the more technical areas of psychology including the study of sensation, motivation, cognition, memory, problem solving, affect, perception, learning or animal behavior. The popular press rarely mentions psychological statistics, personality theory, physiological psychology, industrial and military psychology, or other of the lesser-known interests of psychologists. Much of the popular interest in psychology—and most of the criticism—focuses on counseling, psychotherapy and those parts of the field that deal with personal problems.

Instead of worshiping the God of Abraham, Isaac, Jacob and Jesus, many today bow at the words of Freud, Jung, Rogers, Ellis, Satir, Erhard or whoever is the latest psychological guru. As a new religion, suggests Paul Vitz, psychology has become a cult that worships the self.[4] In place of self-discipline, self-sacrifice, self-denial and self-abasement, the new religion has substituted new values of self-fulfillment, self-actualization, self-realization and the pursuit of self-esteem or a better self-concept. Psychology as religion promises a better life and tells how to get it. It is a religion that has produced thousands of psychologists, psychiatrists and other "new seers"[5] to replace the ministers, priests and rabbis whose influence and counseling effectiveness appear to be fading.

In the opinion of some people, psychology has become a dangerous force that undermines religion, competes with biblical Christianity and delivers its humanistic messages with "the infallible air of a papal bull, a stance which intimidates even the most confident of laymen."[6] It is not surprising that many agree with the popular writer who recently urged the church to "purge itself of psychological theories and terminology, and thus divest itself of the rival religion which it has taken into its bosom."[7]

The Bible clearly instructs believers to keep themselves from idols (1 Jn 5:21). An idol is anything that people worship or depend on apart from God. In ancient times, idols were mostly manmade statues of wood and stone. Today idols are more often manmade conclusions and ideas. Nothing is innately wrong with technology, medical science, new philosophies and contemporary scholarship. All these can be useful and good, but they are destructive when we depend on them solely and when they lead us away from God.

For some people the conclusions of modern psychology have become idols, the basis of a new religion that competes with Christianity.[8] Christians, in contrast, put their hope in the Lord who made heaven and earth and who remains faithful forever (Ps 146:5-6). We do not throw out all psychology simply because some misuse it, any more than we would discard all science or education because some abuse these fields or see them as the only hope for mankind.

In every field of study—psychology included—there are abuses, dangers and errors. The noble people at Berea examined the Scriptures every day to see if Paul's words were true (Acts 17:11). In a similar way, we must examine the messages of modern teachers, including psychology teachers, to see what can be accepted and what must be rejected because it competes with the Word of God.

Some have elevated psychology to the status of a new religion. Some put all their confidence in the insights of psychological teachers and researchers. Some reject Christianity because they are deceived into thinking that a human system of knowledge is more powerful than the

God of the universe. Christians must reject such thinking, just as we reject every other form of idolatry.

But it is simplistic to conclude that all psychology must be rejected because some people have a distorted view of its value. Instead of dismissing all psychology as a rival religion, let us evaluate its findings, learn from them and make use of psychology's insights when they are consistent with Scripture. In this way we can use psychological conclusions to help others deal with the complexities of modern living.

Does Psychology Dabble in the Demonic?

ITS BEEN QUOTED MANY TIMES.
Probably you've read it more than once.

Nevertheless the famous C. S. Lewis statement about the devil is worth repeating. "There are two equal and opposite errors into which our race can fall about the devils," Lewis wrote in his preface to *The Screwtape Letters*. "One is to disbelieve in their existence. The other is to believe, and to feel an excessive and unhealthy interest in them. They themselves are equally pleased by both errors."[1]

As a group, psychologists overwhelmingly fall into the first of Lewis's two categories. Claiming to be neutral scientists with no interest in the supernatural and no reason to study the demonic, most psychologists tend to assume that devils are nonexistent. If demons do exist, say these psychologists, then demonic forces would certainly be of no interest to a science that studies human and animal behavior.

In contrast, some theological critics of psychology fall into Lewis's second category. Convinced that psychology is an agent of the devil, they try to show that psychological methods, concepts and conclusions are channels through which Satanic, occult and Eastern mystical influences enter Western society. Recognizing the power of the demonic, these people take "an excessive and unhealthy interest" in the devil and his forces. Satan is blamed for everything that goes wrong, including most illnesses. New, threatening or unfamiliar ideas (including psychological ideas) are labeled "demonic" and quickly rejected.

Are these views valid? What can we say about psychology and the demonic?

First, *there is evidence that occult practices have been accepted by a large and perhaps growing number of psychological professionals.* Several years ago clinical psychologist Ralph Metzner observed that I Ching, Tantra, Tarot, alchemy, astrology and other occult practices could be useful for producing mental health and giving meaning to life.[2] Another has suggested that "a large and growing number of psychiatrists are now convinced that the Eastern religions offer an understanding of the mind far more complete than anything yet envisaged by Western science."[3] More recently, Christian psychologist William Kirk Kilpatrick argued that Carl Rogers was a "quiet revolutionary" whose ideas and methods introduced a number of occult ideas into mainstream psychology.[4]

Modern human beings, like people of all ages, have a spiritual void and a need for the supernatural. Having turned from the God of the Bible, many people hope to fill the void by looking to biorhythms, reincarnation, astrology, ESP, Eastern meditation, altered states of consciousness and even UFOs or extraterrestial beings. Some appear to be combining elements of psychotherapy and religion with all kinds of occult beliefs and practices.[5] These are indeed disturbing trends in society and in some corners of the psychological profession.

Second, *many who fear the entrance of occult practices into psychology nevertheless draw invalid and illogical conclusions about current counseling practices.* In their often sincere desires to purge occult influences from counseling, some writers have condemned visualization, self-talk, the healing of memories and other frequently used therapeutic methods. These have been labeled "occultist," and even their Christian advocates are described as misguided and deceived.

These are serious allegations. If they are true, then psychology is indeed a more dangerous force than most people suspect.

But the critics undercut many of their conclusions by making errors in logic. Consider the following, for example:

Because all A is B, it does not follow that all B is A.

Because all elephants (A) are animals (B), it does not follow that all animals (B) are elephants (A).

Because all occultists (A) may use visualization (B), it does not follow that all visualization (B) is occultic (A).

Visualization, imagination and guided imagery are related words that describe the use of mental pictures to bring increased understanding, relaxation or self-confidence. The job-seeker who imagines what an interview will be like is using visualization to prepare for the actual meeting with a prospective employer. The tense businessman who relaxes by imagining himself on a quiet beach is using visualization to calm down. The Christian uses visualization when he or she imagines what heaven may be like, ponders how the prodigal son must have felt, or thinks of Christ as being like a hen gathering her chicks under her wings (Mt 23:37).

I agree that some counselors misuse visualization and guided imagery,[6] but this does not mean these practices are wrong in themselves. Some cult leaders, occult practitioners and Eastern mystics use prayer, preaching and even meditation on the Bible, but we don't dismiss these as occultic simply because they are misused by deceived individuals.

Another example of poor logic is the following:

Some A is Satanic. You use some A. Therefore what you use is Satanic.

Some healing-of-memories techniques are Satanic. You use some healing-of-memories techniques. Therefore what you are doing is Satanic.

The more valid statement would be the following:

Some A is bad (occultic). Some A is not bad (not occultic). You use A. Therefore what you use may or may not be bad.

Some self-talk is harmful (depending on what is said). Some self-talk is not harmful (depending on what is said). You use self-talk. Therefore, your self-talk may or may not be harmful.

When self-talk involves telling ourselves things that are unbiblical and untrue, then self-talk is bad. When, in contrast, we talk to ourselves about Scripture, tell ourselves things that are valid or use self-encouragement, then self-talk can be helpful.[7]

Healing of memories—the practice of thinking back over past experiences and asking God to heal hurts and bitterness—can be harmful if it dwells on old, best-forgotten issues, relies on the power of suggestion to cope with problems, becomes an emotion-arousing tactic in mass meetings or is viewed as a self-help gimmick that prevents Christians from confessing sin and committing their lives to Christ. As David Seamands and others have shown, however, the healing of memories can be an effective, biblically based and Christ-honoring way to find lasting help for problems.[8] Our goal as Christians is to "throw off everything that hinders and the sin that so easily entangles" so we can "run with perseverance the race marked out for us" and "fix our eyes on Jesus" (Heb 12:1-2).

Like all believers, Christian counselors must be alert to Satanic influences that can subtly permeate their work and lives. This is our third major point. No Christian can take the devil for granted. Each of us is in a struggle, "not against flesh and blood, but against the rulers, against the authorities, against the powers of this dark world and against the spiritual forces of evil in the heavenly realms" (Eph 6:12).

The devil is not a ferocious-looking, readily identifiable creature with a bright red suit, long tail and pitchfork. He goes about masquerading as an angel of light (2 Cor 11:14). He is a prowler who seeks to devour unsuspecting people. He is like a lion that tears apart its prey (1 Pet 5:8). It is no wonder that the Scriptures tell us to be constantly on the alert (v. 8), to "resist him" (v. 9), to rely on the full armor of God that enables us to stand against the devil's schemes (Eph 6:10-11).

The critics of psychology have served the useful purpose of alerting us to oft-ignored dangers that can and do seep in to the "bag of techniques" used by Christian and non-Christian counselors. Surely it is better to be overly sensitive to Satanic forces than to be blissfully unaware of their influence and existence.

Christian counselors try to keep abreast of current counseling methods and psychological trends. But each of us—psychologist and non-psychologist alike—must be alert so that we do not fall unwittingly into the trap of dabbling in the demonic.

Does Psychology Explain Away Biblical Miracles?

20

PSYCHOLOGIST ALLEN BERGIN MUST BE A COURAGEOUS MAN. AT A PROFESSIONAL convention several years ago he spoke about psychologists and religious experience.

When secular psychologists encounter faith healing, conversion, demon oppression or other religious phenomena, they attempt to classify or explain what they have seen. If that doesn't work, suggested Bergin, psychologists refuse to accept the evidence. It is as if an entomologist, having discovered a new insect he couldn't classify, were to step on it.

There is at least some truth in Bergin's observation. Few psychologists pay much attention to religious experience, but when they do, they attempt to explain it psychologically. If that fails, they may "step on" the experience—dismiss it as improbable and therefore nonexistent. Philosopher David Hume reached a similar conclusion over two centuries ago. In an argument that modern philosophers have refuted, Hume proclaimed that miracles are impossible since they violate the laws of nature.[1] Many modern psychologists would agree.

A miracle can be defined as an unusual event that has no known natural explanation but is assumed to result from the intervention of some supernatural power. According to C. S. Lewis, the greatest miracle of all was the Incarnation, when God's Son humbled himself and came to earth in the form of a man.[2] Jesus Christ in turn performed miracles that could be classified in several categories: miracles of fertility (feeding the multitudes or turning water into wine), miracles of destruction (causing the fig tree to wither), miracles of dominion over the inorganic (calming a storm), miracles of reversal (the raising of Lazarus), miracles of perfecting or glorification (his own resurrection) and miracles of healing. The healing miracles are the ones that most interest psychologists. To some extent this is because healing deals with people. Perhaps these miracles also are easiest to classify and explain psychologically.

Some psychologists have been quick to point out that reports about the frequency and extent of healing are likely to be biased and exaggerated. Faithful believers see what they want to see and give testimonials that don't always hold up to careful investigation. The Catholic shrine at Lourdes in France is visited by thousands of people every year. Many claim to have been healed there, but even the Catholic Church acknowledges that real healings are much rarer than faithful believers maintain.[3] Similar conclusions followed the ministry of healer Kathryn Kuhlmann.[4]

There is evidence that some healings result from deliberate deception. Con artists, ancient and modern, may trick people into believing that healing has occurred. Many of the psychic surgeons in the Philippines would fit this category,[5] and so might some unethical evangelists and modern North American healers.

Some healings result from what is called the *placebo effect*. Given placebos (capsules that contain no medicines), sick people often improve even though they have received no drugs or other medical treatment, apparently because the mind contributes to physical healing.[6] In such cases the body is mobilized by the mere belief that an effective treatment has been given. This belief activates the endocrine system, which then produces chemical changes that bring healing. Faith in the power of a placebo or a healer can actually bring healing. Belief in the power of prayer might stimulate a similar physical reaction.

Perhaps more common among psychologists is the conclusion that many healings are related to psychologically produced sicknesses known as *conversion reactions*—physical illnesses brought on by psychological tension. If religion reduces stress, gives the patient new hope or provides a reason for living, then psychological tension fades and psychosomatic illnesses and symptoms disappear. Psychologists can explain this naturally, without having to believe in miracles and without being tempted to stamp out things that appear to be supernatural.

But how do we explain the raising of Lazarus, the lame men in the Bible who walked, the recovery of Jairus's daughter, the blind who were made to see or the previously violent, mentally deranged people who sat clothed, at peace and in their right minds after meeting Jesus? Are these examples of biased reporting by ignorant prescientific writers? Are they evidence of misperception, misunderstanding or misreporting?

"We all have Naturalism in our bones," C. S. Lewis once observed. We are impressed by scholars who "make it part of their method to eliminate the supernatural whenever it is even remotely possible to do so, to strain natural explanation even to the breaking point before they admit the least suggestion of miracle."[7] Sometimes the naturalistic psychological explanations of faith healing and other miracles are harder to believe than the actual existence of supernatural happenings.

"You must develop a nose like a blood-hound for those steps in the argument which depend not on historical and linguistic knowledge but on the concealed assumption that miracles are impossible, improbable, or improper."[8]

The Christian does not ignore these psychological critiques even when they come from people convinced that miracles are impossible. Psychological insights often help us understand so-called miraculous events more clearly. Psychological conclusions prevent us from believing exaggerated and invalid reports of healings and other miracles. The skepticism of those firmly wedded to naturalism can help us get a clearer perspective on events assumed to be miraculous.

But psychological explanations cannot account for all miracles, and the Christian is left with at least three conclusions:

First, God is able to do miracles, including healing. That was true in Bible times and it is true today. Even though some of these events can be at least partially understood (and thus do not completely fit the definition of miracles), there still are supernatural events that defy human understanding and doubtless will continue to do so (Rom 11:33). Despite our understanding of the healing process, we still are commanded to pray for the sick and to expect that healing can and often will come from God—supernaturally and in his timing (Jas 5:15).

Second, the Christian realizes that Satan and his demonic forces may also bring healing. As we have seen, the devil is able to display "all kinds of counterfeit miracles, signs and wonders" that delude many people (2 Thess 2:9-11). Could this include healing? Several insightful writers have argued that the answer is yes.[9] These demonic miracles cannot be explained psychologically, and neither are they the result of God's divine intervention. They are miracles that come, instead, from the devil.

Third, even when miracles can be explained psychologically, God may still be involved. Freud reached the mistaken conclusion that advancing scientific explanations ultimately would cause religious "illusions" to disappear.[10] But increased knowledge and better understanding does not eliminate God. Instead it gives us greater understanding of the complexities of the marvelous universe he has created and holds together by his power (Heb 1:1-3).

The psychological study of healings and other miracles is not something the Christian should criticize or avoid. Such study can strengthen our faith in the all-powerful God who has the ability to work those miracles we probably never will understand, but for which we can give praise and thanksgiving.[11]

That's a lot better than trying to step on something we don't like or can't classify.

Are Psychological Problems All Caused By Sin?

21

I KNOW AN UNUSUAL MAN WHO HAS A STRING OF DOCTOR'S DEGREES LISTED after his name. He began by getting an M.D. Then he passed the examinations to become a psychiatrist and went on to get a doctorate in psychology. One or two colleges gave him honorary doctorates, but he still was motivated to enroll in a theological seminary where he eventually earned a doctor's degree in theology. This brilliant man now has more letters in his list of doctorates than most of us have in our names.

In speaking to a group of pastors, the well-doctored gentleman once expressed his opinion about who really is competent to counsel.

"Since so many problems have a physical basis," he began, "only medically trained people should counsel.

"But physicians are mostly trained to deal with physical problems, so they shouldn't counsel unless they have added training in psychiatry or psychology."

The speaker was not finished.

"Many problems have a spiritual basis," he continued. "For this reason, I believe the truly competent counselor must also be theologically trained."

The members of the audience must have felt discouraged and inadequate after this speech. The man with all the doctorates had stated that without medical, psychological and theological training, nobody should counsel. He had eliminated almost everybody from the field of counseling—except himself.

This is an extreme view, but some of us with fewer, different or no academic degrees reach similar conclusions.

Freud was willing to admit that nonphysicians could learn and practice psychoanalysis, but he didn't think anyone was competent to counsel until he or she had completed hundreds of hours of psychoanalysis and analytic training.

Many modern physicians believe that only medically trained people are competent to counsel. Psychologists, as you might expect, disagree, and one pastoral counselor takes an even different view. "A good seminary education rather than medical school or a degree in clinical psychology, is the most fitting background for a counselor," he suggests. "Christian counselors properly trained in the Scriptures are competent to counsel—more competent than psychiatrists or anyone else."[1]

These contrasting conclusions come, in part, because we have different opinions about the causes of human problems.[2] If problems are caused mostly by physical or psychological influences, then pastors or lay people are not qualified to counsel. If problems are ultimately spiritual, then Christians alone should counsel.

Are all personal problems "nothing but" spiritual problems? Three observations can help us find an answer.

All problems are the result of original sin. According to the first page in the Old Testament, God created males and females in the divine image—and what he created was good (Gen 1:27, 31). Very soon, however, the first humans disobeyed God, fell into sin, and were introduced to the physical pain and mental turmoil that has been our lot ever since.

Since all problems come ultimately from that original sin, it is in one sense valid to say that, at root, all psychological problems are spiritual. If a person gets depressed, for example, we could conclude that depression was caused by the Fall and therefore is nothing but a spiritual problem. As we will see, however, depression and most other forms of emotional distress cannot be explained away so simply.

All problems have a mental, physical and spiritual component. Martin and Deidre Bobgan state this concisely and accurately:

There has been an unfortunate division of mind and body. What generally happens is that the medical doctor's main interest is with the body and the psychotherapist's with the mind. The separation of mind from body is a naive way of dealing with the total person. In fact, the total person also includes the spirit. The body, mind and the spirit must be considered in any problem which a person is experiencing. . . . Any system which regards one, such as the body or the mind, without considering all three, and particularly the spiritual part of man, falls short of truly ministering to the whole person.[3]

There is abundant evidence that all human problems have three components: physical, psychological and spiritual.[4] Sometimes one of these may be most noticeable and in greatest need of treatment, but each is influenced by the other two.

Depression, for example, may have a strictly physical cause; it may be a biochemical reaction to illness or some other body malfunction. Other depression may come as a reaction to stress such as the loss of a loved one or failure in a job. As we have seen earlier, depression can also come from sin. The complexity of depressive reactions shows the inaccuracy of concluding that psychological problems are nothing but spiritual problems.

All "nothing buttery" thinking is overly simplistic. At times it is easy for all of us to think that one issue may be *nothing but* an indication of something else. Freud thought like this when he said that God is *nothing but* an illusion. Some writers have suggested that Paul's conversion on the Damascus road was *nothing but* a sunstroke or epileptic seizure. Perhaps there are still those who believe that persisting personal problems are *nothing but* a lack of faith. Does this same kind of thinking lead others to conclude that psychological problems are *nothing but* spiritual issues?

Christian psychologist Lawrence Crabb has summarized the nothing-buttery philosophy as it often appears in the church.[5] It starts with the valid conclusion that God has given everything we need to know about living effectively (2 Pet 1:3). It assumes that a careful study of the Scriptures will enable us to discover God's principles for living. From this it concludes that personal problems are *nothing but* a failure to live in accordance with divine principles. The counselor, it is assumed, needs to know *nothing but* Scripture. Counseling involves *nothing but* confronting people with their sin and challenging them to live in accordance with the biblical principles. Helping is naively assumed to be "no more complicated than finding wrong behaviors, instructing people *what* they should do differently, and planning, exhorting, and demanding appropriate changes."[6]

Let us return once again to our example of depression. The effective Christian counselor knows that personal sin may be a major cause of depression, but it would be simplistic to conclude that treatment should include nothing but finding the sin and exhorting the person to change. Sometimes it is necessary to uncover and treat the physical causes of depression. At times we need to help the counselee cope with his or her psychological stress. Effective people-helping cannot not rest on nothing-buttery thinking.

Viktor Frankl, the famous Austrian psychiatrist, once spoke about the ways in which we could view a drinking glass. Viewed from the top, from an angle and from the side, the glass seems to take on three different shapes, even though it doesn't actually change.

In a similar way, we can view human beings from a spiritual, psychological or physical perspective. Each gives a slightly different viewpoint. Each is partially right, but none gives the complete picture.

It is invalid to conclude that all spiritual problems are nothing but physical illnesses that must be seen and treated from a medical perspective. It is equally invalid to assume that all psychological problems are nothing but spiritual problems that can be treated only by a pastor or trained theologian.

Can Christians Study Secular Psychology without Undermining Their Faith?

Near the beginning of my first year in graduate school, I was delighted to discover several other Christian students in the psychology department. We went to different churches, but we shared similar beliefs and talked on occasion about our common desire to provide effective Christian counseling following our years of professional training.

One of the students, a young minister, divorced his wife a few months later, married a secretary and quit the church. Another decided that psychology had greater sophistication than his "simple faith," so he also left the church and forsook Christianity. A third was a social climber who concluded that the Christian lifestyle is an impediment to any person who wants to get to the top.

I hesitate to mention the church dropout rate of my graduate-school classmates. A departure from the faith doesn't always occur among psychologists, but sometimes it does. The question that heads this chapter is important, especially for Christian students.

Most psychology students know about Freud's little book, *The Future of an Illusion*.[1] In its sixty pages, the founder of psychoanalysis dismisses religion as an illusion comparable to a childhood neurosis. With the advance of science, including psychological science, Freud hoped that the "universal obsessional neurosis" of religion would eventually fade away.

Freud's successors tended to be more sympathetic toward religion, but few had any desire to propagate the ancient God-given faith of Abraham, Isaac and Jacob. Carl Jung, for example, was a mystic whose writings in places would be considered blatant heresy by most Christians. Erich Fromm appeared to have a slightly better understanding of traditional religion, but he proposed that it be replaced by an atheistic religion of humanism. There would be no submission to authority in this new religion that Fromm proposed. Love would be emphasized, and God would be seen not as the compassionate sovereign Lord but merely as a symbol of human powers.[2]

It would be unfair to blame this rise of humanistic heresy solely on the works of psychoanalysts and psychologists. In the 1950s, several books described the appearance of what has been called "American Religion."[3] This was an empty, largely meaningless religion with no explicit doctrines or theology, little intellectual content, few standards of right and wrong, no submission to any authority, but frequent talk about love, good will and togetherness. American religion emphasized practical achievement, had "every confidence in the rightness of its intentions" and tended to react against those who might call that rightness into question.[4] It had a vague view of God and saw him as manageable, cozy, good tempered and captive to the demands and whims of those inclined to use him.[5] It was a religion that went far beyond psychology but was not reluctant to embrace psychological concepts and ideas.

It is easy to understand how contact with this new American religion and its psychological counterparts could undercut the faith of young or immature Christians. According to psychologist Paul Vitz, a Christian who teaches in a secular university, "psychologists today are indifferent to Christianity because they rarely hear it advocated in their professional environment; when it is brought to their attention the hostility is clear."[6] It isn't easy for students to keep the faith when they meet indifference or hostility from psychology teachers and other students.

There can be no denial that much of psychology is more than indifferent to religion; it is opposed to religion. Like most other people in our society, many psychologists have no belief in a personal God, no acceptance of biblical authority, no desire to obey biblical standards of morality, no interest in understanding Christian teachings and often no tolerance of believers. These antibiblical views may in fact be held more frequently by psychologists than by other professionals.[7] Many psychologists and psychotherapists do understand, respect and tolerate people who are deeply religious, but a sizable percentage tend to be intolerant and opposed to religion, especially Christianity.

Even with all their criticisms, however, psychologists still have an interest in religion. Freud, Jung, Fromm, Maslow, James, Skinner, Rogers and a host of others criticized religion but then went on to propose alternatives. Regrettably, many of the alternatives have been in the form of Eastern religions that seek to undermine Christianity.[8]

If psychologists are guilty of opposing, undermining and sometimes attempting to replace traditional religious beliefs with empty humanistic substitutes, shouldn't Christians flee from them? Paul instructed Timothy to "turn away from godless chatter and the opposing ideas of what is falsely called knowledge, which some have professed and in so doing have wandered from the faith" (1 Tim 6:20-21). Is this what happened to my fellow psychology students in graduate school?

Elsewhere Paul writes that it is Christ "in whom are hidden all the treasures of wisdom and knowledge. I tell you this so that no one may deceive you by fine-sounding arguments. . . . See to it that no one takes you captive through hollow and deceptive philosophy, which depends on human tradition and the basic principles of this world rather than on Christ" (Col 2:3-4, 8.)

How, then, does the Christian respond to psychology and this clear teaching of Scripture? First, a Christian who studies psychology must pay attention to spiritual growth. Before warning against deceptive worldly philosophies, Paul instructs believers, "Just as you received Christ Jesus as Lord, continue to live in him, rooted and built up in him, strengthened in the faith as you were taught, and overflowing with thankfulness" (Col 2:6-7). Regular times of meditation on Scripture, worship with other believers, and consistent prayer that includes thanksgiving can all strengthen believers and protect them from harmful influences that come not just from psychology but from all corners of society.

Second, the Christian psychology student must be alert, recognizing that even committed believers can be deceived by fine-sounding arguments and human tradition. The alert Christian goes through life remembering the admonition that "if you think you are standing firm, be careful that you don't fall" (1 Cor 10:12). Alert believers know that "God is faithful; he will not let you be tempted beyond what you can bear. But when you are tempted, he will also provide a way out so that you can stand up under it" (1 Cor 10:13). We aren't likely to see the "way out," however, if we become insensitive to the danger of temptation.

Third, the Christian must recognize that psychology, like every other field of study, can be helpful—providing it is tested against the revealed Word of God. Christians do not accept all of psychology uncritically. Like everything else in life, psychology must be brought under the authority of the Bible. Psychology can be received gratefully and studied enthusiastically when it is consistent with biblical teaching. In contrast, parts of psychology must be rejected if they contradict or attempt to undermine scriptural truths.

I have wondered on occasion why I never abandoned the church or turned away from Christ during my years of graduate training in psychology. Clearly God was protecting—and no doubt answering the prayers of those who were concerned about my life and spiritual welfare. That same God also led me to make private devotions a high priority even when there were papers and projects due, to keep involved in a local church, to be alert to temptation and to study psychology with a constant awareness that the science of human behavior could be both powerfully effective and subtly dangerous.

Psychology, like thousands of other influences in this world, can and sometimes does undermine the faith of Christians. But that doesn't have to happen. Becoming a hermit or a psychological illiterate is not the answer to temptation. Part of the answer comes in learning to discriminate between what is harmful and what can be helpful. The ultimate answer comes in seeking divine protection, in growing spiritually and in recognizing that those who think they stand should be alert so they don't fall.

Why Is Psychology Taught In Seminaries and Bible Colleges?

23

I DO IT ONCE OR TWICE EVERY YEAR. ARMED WITH A BRIEFCASE FULL OF LECTURE notes and throat lozenges, I jump on a plane and take off to a distant college or seminary to give their annual lectures.

These lectureships are usually paid for by some wealthy alumnus, enthusiastically promoted by the administration, tolerated by the professors and hated by the students. I sometimes accept the whole experience as a challenge—to be interesting, humorous and practical in spite of everybody's expectations that the lectures will be pompous, ponderous and dull. Early in my career, I discovered that being a guest lecturer can be tiring, stimulating and a lot of fun.

Recently, for example, I visited a seminary campus for a week, lectured every day in chapel, spoke in an endless succession of classes, was a guest on the local radio station and had every meal with a different professor or group of students. The last meeting of the week was a class where students were expected to ask questions.

"Why should psychology be taught on a seminary campus?" one of the theological students asked. The professor was enthusiastic about psychology as a field of study, but even he could think of no good reason for teaching this subject in a graduate school that existed to train people for the ministry.

My mind went immediately to a fund-raising letter that had come recently from the president of another seminary. "The architecture of our campus centers around the chapel," the letter began. "This is as it should be because the heart of the ministry is preaching. The goal of our school is to make good preachers."

Every committed Christian and seminary professor agrees that preaching is important. Preaching is a central part of the minister's work; it is a crucial part of pastoral education. Jesus emphasized preaching by his own teaching and example. Peter, John, Paul and all the well-known leaders in the early church were powerful preachers.

But they were more than preachers.

They cared for the sick, encouraged the downhearted, prayed for fellow believers, evangelized through private conversations, taught individuals and small groups, wrote letters of instruction and counsel, bore each other's burdens and shared with one another. Preaching was important, but so was a more private ministry that included healing.

When Jesus educated the first ministerial candidates—his disciples—he gave them spiritual preparation, specific instructions for their ministries, warnings about the dangers they would face, encouragement to sustain them in their work and practical experience (Mt 10:5-20). He sent them "to preach the kingdom of God and to heal the sick" (Lk 9:2). Preaching was no more or less important than healing. When the disciples returned from their practicum experience, Jesus welcomed them back, spoke to them about God's kingdom and healed those who needed healing (Lk 9:11).

Ministerial preparation that teaches people how to preach but fails to teach them how to heal is only half an education. It ignores half the biblical model for theological education.

From this does it follow that psychology is needed? Doesn't healing deal with the body? If nontheologians are to join the teaching faculty, wouldn't it be better to bring in a physician rather than a psychologist?

In the Bible, healing involves "restoration to a state of health."[1] Such restoration refers to physical healing, but it also applies to spiritual healing and healing of the mind. When the demon-possessed man was healed, for example, his behavior changed, and people were amazed to see that he was "in his right mind" (Lk 8). When the Lord healed the paralytic, the people were critical and surprised because Jesus dealt with the man's need for spiritual healing before telling him to get up and walk (Mt 9:1-8). Jesus healed spiritual, mental, interpersonal and physical hurts.

Some who agree with this conclusion might still argue that psychology has no place in a school of theology.[2] Counseling and healing of the mind are theological issues, these critics maintain, and they are best addressed by students of the Bible.

There is no place in a theological school for psychological teaching that ignores or contradicts the Scriptures. Divine revelation is our ultimate source of authority, and all scientific conclusions must be consistent with the revealed Word of God. Just as God-given medical facts and methods can contribute to healing, however, so can the many conclusions from disciplines such as sociology and psychology. Surely such fields of study should not be barred from theological schools.

As a study of human behavior, psychology prepares a person not only to counsel but also to mediate disputes, motivate volunteers, communicate effectively, lead group discussions, empathize with the hurting and serve spiritual meat in an appealing fashion. All these (and no doubt more) are reasons to teach principles of human behavior to seminarians.

Equally important is the need for Christian students to understand the apologetical implications of psychology. Apologetics is a branch of theology that exists to defend the faith against its accusers.[3] It is a response to Peter's statement that Christians should "always be prepared to give an answer to everyone who asks you to give the reason for the hope that you have." We are to do this with gentleness and respect (1 Pet 3:15-16).

Some of the more powerful questions and attacks today come from nonbelievers who try to explain away religion by using psychological arguments. These arguments can and should be answered and refuted, but often they seem to be ignored, even in apologetics classes. Who is better equipped than a Christian psychologist to teach students how to keep the faith in the midst of psychological challenges?

There have been times and places where psychology has replaced theological or biblical studies and become the core of the curriculum. This is wrong. Theological schools exist primarily to teach the Bible, theology and practical Christianity. But a biblically sensitive psychology can play an important role in seminary and Bible college training. To cast psychology aside is to throw out a valuable resource for helping us understand, evangelize, help, heal and enlighten both believers and non-Christians.

Can Secular Psychology and Christianity Be Integrated?

*C*AN CHRISTIANITY AND PSYCHOLOGY MIX?

Does the study of psychology water down the Christian's spiritual commitment?

Is psychology in competition with Scripture?

When I was a freshman taking my first course in psychology, these questions never crossed my mind; but among Christian students of psychology today, few topics are more controversial or debated with as much vehemence.

"Christian leaders should stop trying to *integrate* (the great buzz word of eclectic Christian counselors) biblical teaching with these systems that offer so little promise," wrote one observer who has little respect for modern psychology.[1]

"True Christianity does not mix well with psychology," wrote another.[2] Try to mix them, and "you often end up with a watered-down Christianity instead of a Christianized psychology."[3] Attempt to reconcile the two, and psychology will ultimately "have the effect of undermining the Christian point of view."[4]

Television evangelist Jimmy Swaggart has written with even stronger conviction: "Is it possible to merge biblical and clinical counseling? Is it possible to unite the Ark of the Covenant with Baal? Is it possible to join the Levitical priesthood with the Philistines in the service of the temple?" Efforts to integrate psychology and Christianity involve "an impossible feat of surgery: to graft secular humanistic beliefs onto those of the Bible. This will never work."[5]

How different is the opinion of psychologist and seminary professor Craig Ellison. "For a growing number of Christians and non-Christians," he writes, "the rigorous study of relationships between psychology and religion in general (and Christianity in particular) is an important and legitimate activity."[6]

How does the committed Christian respond to these strong differences of opinion? Can—and should—secular psychology be integrated with Christian beliefs?

Integration is not always understood. Some critics seem to assume that integrating psychology and Christianity involves attempting to merge two equal systems of thought. This is impossible, the critics argue. It is like trying to mix oil and water.

Since taking that freshman course many years ago, I have read widely on the subject of integration.[7] Never do I recall committed Christian psychologists suggesting that integration is the same as merger. For the Christian psychologist, integration involves a recognition of the ultimate authority of the Bible, a willingness to learn what God has allowed humans to discover through psychology and other fields of knowledge, and a desire to determine how both scriptural truths and psychological data can enable us better to understand and help people.

Integration makes no attempt to elevate psychology to the level of the Word of God. Integration does not try to recast theology in psychological terms, water down or contradict the truths of Scripture, infiltrate the church and weaken the gospel message, or substitute methods of psychology for the work of the Holy Spirit. Integration instead refers to "the uniting, but not the fusing, of psychology and theology. Integration is the process whereby both disciplines retain their own identity while benefiting from each other's perspective and communicating the same truth."[8]

The Christian in psychology, like all other believers, constantly asks how his or her knowledge of Scripture and relationship with Jesus Christ infiltrates and affects every area of life, study and work. To divide life into parts—physical, mental, psychological, spiritual; family, work, worship, leisure—is to chop human existence into pieces and to deny that we are holistic beings controlled and influenced by the Sovereign God of the universe.

Integration is not always wise. It is well known that parts of psychology clearly contradict Scripture and could never be accepted by or integrated into the Christian's conclusions and work. Some psychological techniques are clearly immoral. Some psychological conclusions reflect more of Eastern mysticism than of scientific research. Some research data is inconclusive and too speculative to be accepted by Christians. Psychological conclusions that contradict biblical principles certainly cannot be integrated with Christianity.

Integration is not always easy. Every fall I teach a course on integration. Each year a few students expect to learn some formula for neatly tying psychology and Christianity together.

There are no such formulas.[9]

In one sense, integrating psychology with theology is like trying to compare European language with Asian language. There are dozens of European and Asian languages, just as there are a variety of psychological and theological conclusions and perspectives. Integration is not as simple as it might at first appear.

It is important, therefore, that integration be done carefully, selectively, tentatively and by individuals who seek to be led by the Holy Spirit. Several years ago in a talk about integration I made the following comments. They still reflect my thinking today:

I am committed intellectually to the task of integration. I want it to be reflected in my work, my writing, and my teaching. Most of all, however, I want my theology and my psychology to be integrated in my life—not compartmentalized into separate noninteracting categories. . . . I believe that the integration of psychology and theology is an important intellectual challenge. I believe that integration must have practical applications. But I believe even more that integration must start and be reflected in the mind and behavior of the integrator.[10]

Integration is not always avoidable. It is comfortable to assume that all moral issues can be divided into clear right and clear wrong with no confusing uncertainties in between. It would be wonderful if all theology could be separated into clear truth versus clear error with no areas of disagreement or uncertainty in between. It would be convenient if all counseling could be divided neatly into "the psychological way" and "the spiritual way" with no overlapping goals, methods or assumptions.

But life is never this simple. Even those who try to dichotomize counseling into psychological versus biblical approaches have to admit that there is overlap. Listening, talking, confessing, accepting, thinking and understanding are neither purely psychological nor exclusively biblical activities.[11] Even love, hope, compassion, forgiveness, caring, kindness, confrontation and a host of other concepts are shared by theologians and psychologists. The person who wants to understand and help others cannot avoid at least some overlap and integration of psychological and Christian principles.

Integration is not always wrong. Scientists occasionally write about Galileo who in 1615 was called before the Inquisition at Rome because he believed in the Copernican theory that the earth is not the center of the universe. That the sun does not revolve around the earth was at the time called "foolish, absurd, false in theology, and heretical, . . . expressly contrary to Holy Scripture . . . and from a theological point of view at least, opposed to the true faith."[12]

The Word of God is true and unchanging. But human interpretations change, and sometimes theologies are found to be in error while the findings of science stand as firm as the Copernican theory. The conclusions of those believers who attempt to integrate psychology and theology may in time appear not nearly so heretical as some modern believers suggest.

Scholarly work to date has shown, however, that Christians and psychologists can learn from each other, without weakening or watering down the enduring truths of God's Word. Certainly this can be done without weakening the spiritual commitment of the searcher who accepts God's Word and learns from the study of God's creation. It is too early to answer decisively if psychology and Christianity can be integrated. But for too many sincere believers, the future of this endeavor looks promising.

PART FOUR
Questions about Special Issues

Is Mental Illness a Myth?

25

DR. THOMAS SZASZ IS NO ORDINARY PSYCHIATRIST. BORN IN BUDAPEST, HUNgary, he moved to the United States in 1938 at age twenty, became a psychoanalyst, spent a period of time with the United States Navy and settled in upstate New York where he became a university professor of psychiatry.

Soon the professor began writing articles and books that stirred up a caldron of controversy. In *The Myth of Mental Illness* Szasz argued that there is no such thing as mental illness, that traditional treatment is often more harmful than helpful and that disturbed individuals suffer not from illness, but from "problems in living."[1]

Centuries ago, what we now call mental disorder or abnormal behavior was treated by the clergy. In a period that surely is one of the darkest spots in church history, well-meaning but seemingly sadistic theologians tortured thousands of mentally deranged people in an attempt to drive out demons and eliminate "lunacy." Humanitarian reforms began in the late 1700s, but apart from Quakers and a few other religious groups, the changes came from outside the church. Increasing numbers of physicians began to argue that the psychologically deranged were really "mentally ill" people who needed qualified medical treatment rather than torturous exorcisms.

By the early twentieth century, psychiatry and other branches of the medical profession had taken control of treatment. Abnormal behavior was widely accepted as an illness that could be treated only by physicians.

Thomas Szasz was not the only one to challenge this notion,[2] but he was probably the most controversial critic. "It is customary to define psychiatry as a medical specialty concerned with the study, diagnosis, and treatment of mental illnesses," he wrote. "This is a worthless and misleading definition. Mental illness is a myth."[3]

According to Szasz, this idea of mental illness encourages people to think that all problems are physically caused, that we have no responsibility for coping with our own problems and that change comes only to those who passively accept their doctors' treatment. A more recent variation on the same theme has come from psychiatrist Garth Wood, whose previously mentioned book, *The Myth of Neurosis*, has a revealing subtitle: *Overcoming the Illness Excuse.*[4]

As we might expect, the writings of such critics have not been well received by professional counselors. Some of their counselees are equally distressed. "It bothers me to read such books," a former student confessed recently. "I've been seeing a therapist for almost two years, and it confuses me to read that my problems might really be excuses that keep me from facing responsibility."

Is mental illness really a myth? Is it a mind game[5] that allows professional counselors to believe in "the myth of psychotherapy"[6] and gives their counselees an excuse to avoid responsibility while doing nothing about the problems of living?

To answer, let us first agree that *some* abnormal behavior is physically caused. Distorted thinking, emotional disturbances, unusual behavior and many of the other symptoms we call "mental illness" can and often do have a physiological basis. Most psychotherapists and their critics agree that biological disease or other physiological malfunctioning can lead to mental distress and "psychiatric illness." These mental illnesses are not myths.

From this it does not follow, however, that *all* symptoms of abnormality have a physical cause. Many problems have no apparent physical origin but come instead from stress, misperceptions, faulty learning, personality characteristics, lack of social and other skills, or unhealthy attitudes that may have been implanted many years ago. Sometimes people see these in themselves and are able to do something to improve. More often we need the insights and encouragement of others—including professional counselors—who can help us see things differently and give support as we take responsibility for making changes.

Have you ever felt trapped by some habit you couldn't shake—perpetual procrastination, nail biting, overeating, masturbation, lustful thoughts, worry, overusing credit cards or others? We might try to dismiss these as myths that are of no consequence or as "nothing but spiritual issues." But even among committed believers, habits like these grip and control us in spite of our persistent prayers, creative self-help programs and repeated determination to change. Sometimes we need the insights of another human being to help us understand why these problems hang on despite our best efforts to change. Usually there is a reason for the stubborn persistence of bad habits—a reason that may be neither physical nor spiritual.

I have a friend who recently "flunked out" of college. Terry's test scores show he is intellectually very capable, but he has a great tendency to waste time. This problem has no apparent physical basis, and I am convinced that it is not the result of sin or spiritual laziness. The problem instead appears to have a psychological root.

Terry never had to study in high school and has never learned time management or study skills. His parents gave him little encouragement to study and, even now they see no need for him to go to college. Is it surprising that he has dropped out?

As Christians, we can agree further that "mental symptoms" sometimes arise as the result of sin. David's sin left him physically sick, depressed, weak and overwhelmed with guilt. He felt feeble and utterly crushed, isolated, fearful of plots against his life, numb and too anguished to speak clearly or to understand the words of others. It is true that David was surrounded by "vigorous enemies" when he wrote Psalm 38, but the cause of his mental symptoms is clear: "I confess my iniquity; I am troubled by my sin" (v. 18).

No doubt David would have benefited from medical treatment, counseling and the support of caring friends, but he gave no thought to the possibility that his mental illness might be a myth. Instead, David took responsibility for looking at his life, confessing his sin and calling to the Lord: "Do not forsake me; be not far from me, O my God. Come quickly to help me, O Lord my Savior" (Ps 38:21-22).

Thomas Szasz and his colleagues have done something of value by demystifying much of contemporary counseling and psychotherapy. It is a myth to assume that all major problems or symptoms of emotional and mental disorientation result from mental illness that must be treated by psychiatrists.

But surely it is also overly simplistic, perhaps even a myth, to assume that—

☐ all emotional problems are really problems of living (even though many are);

☐ all emotional problems result from personal sin (even though many do);

☐ all emotional problems can be "treated" by untrained people (even though this is sometimes true);

☐ all emotional problems must be treated by professionals (even though this is sometimes necessary);

☐ all emotional problems are really excuses people use to avoid taking responsibility for life's problems (even though this often happens);

☐ all emotional problems can yield to self-treatment when people are determined to get better (even though this can and does happen);

☐ all emotional problems would disappear if people would only pray, confess their sin and trust God (even though this can and often does reduce or eliminate problems).[7]

For those of us who think clearly and cope with life successfully, it is easy to dismiss "mental illness" as nonexistent, easily solvable or nothing more than problems of living. But that won't be the view of anyone who has been gripped by anxiety, dragged into the depths of depression, locked in a struggle with guilt, faced with the terror of losing contact with reality or helpless in watching as a loved one has become psychologically distraught, intensely afraid or disoriented. For these people, mental distress is very real.

And that's no myth.

Is Psychology Really a Science?

*T*HE FIRST COURSE I EVER TAUGHT IN PSYCHOLOGY WAS GIVEN AT A LITTLE ARMY base in West Germany. Like most beginning instructors, I assigned one textbook for the students to read and used another to prepare my lectures.

All went well until the second class when I stated that psychology was a science. Some of my soldier-students didn't agree. For some reason, psychology seemed far different from the *hard* sciences of physics, chemistry, biology or neurophysiology. My explanation that psychology was a *social-behavioral* science must have been weak because it didn't satisfy everyone. At the time I didn't realize that psychology has been fighting for scientific status almost since its beginning.

Despite nuclear reactor meltdowns, space-shuttle accidents and the failure of artificial hearts, most people seem to have a great respect for science. In the popular mind there is something awesome about men and women in white coats working in large laboratories and discussing weighty matters in technical language that the rest of us don't understand. Facts that have been "proven scientifically" are usually assumed to be true. Research that is "empirical" or "scientific" is thought to be accurate, carefully conducted, largely free from bias and reliable.[1]

Psychological researchers have attempted to apply rigorous scientific standards to the study of behavior. But it is difficult to use scientific methods to study emotions like love and hope, the behavior of street gangs, the religious experiences of churchgoers or the effectiveness of psychotherapy. Many creative scientific-based methods have been designed in an attempt to accurately measure and test psychological concepts. But none of these has approached the rigor and seemingly clear-cut methodology of the natural sciences.

When I was a financially struggling graduate student, I found enough money to buy several volumes of a highly acclaimed encyclopedia entitled *Psychology: A Study of a Science.*[2] The editor, a distinguished psychologist named Sigmund Koch, was given funding by the National Science Foundation so he could find eighty scholars who would compile and evaluate the methods, facts and research conclusions of psychology.

Imagine my dismay when Koch later wrote that thirty years of study had led him to conclude that it is "by this time utterly and finally clear that *psychology cannot be a coherent science."* It is "highly unrealistic," Koch suggested, to think that the term *science* could be applied to "perception, cognition, motivation, learning, social psychology, psychopathology, personology, esthetics, the study of creativity" and the other complexities of human behavior.[3] Many of these subdivisions of psychology have been studied scientifically, but it is difficult to pull these together into a coherent body of scientific knowledge.

Must we conclude, then, that psychology is at best a pseudoscience[4] and possibly even a form of superstition or magic?[5]

Before accepting this extreme conclusion we should remind ourselves what all good science attempts to accomplish. First, scientists *observe data* as objectively, thoroughly and accurately as possible. No observation is completely free from bias, but science attempts to control and reduce subjective distortions. Second, scientists seek to *classify data*, organizing it in a meaningful way. Third, scientists attempt to *explain data* in terms of cause-effect relationships. Often this involves formulating, testing and reformulating hypotheses in a repeated series of controlled experiments and careful observations. Scientists hope that eventually their understanding will be so accurate that they can *predict* and even *control* how their subject matter will respond in the future. Many psychologists attempt to follow these guidelines.

This brings us to another conclusion about science: by definition, it is not limited to laboratories and people wearing white coats. In its broadest sense *science* means "knowledge." One dictionary defines science as "knowledge, especially of facts or principles, gained by systematic study; a particular branch of knowledge, especially one dealing with a body of facts or truths systematically arranged and showing the operation of general laws."[6] Such a definition does not limit science to physics or biology. Mathematics, history, psychology and even theology could be considered sciences. Such a definition has let some enthusiastic theologians refer to their discipline as the "queen of the sciences."

Another observation concerns the procedures of science. According to the dictionary, the scientific method is "a research method characterized by the definition of a problem, the gathering of data, and the drafting and empirical testing of the hypothesis."[7] While many psychologists do carefully controlled experimental research, the scientific method does not demand that we limit our studies to experiments. Some subjects that concern psychologists cannot be studied in this way.

Often the psychologist is torn between two approaches. One of these is the intuitive, clinical approach that emphasizes human emotion and behavior in all their *richness*. The other is the exacting, quantitative, experimental approach that emphasizes *precision*.[8] Is the richness approach that "seeks a full, satisfying understanding of an individual" any less or more valid than the "toughminded precisionist" strategy that concentrates on repeatable, observable, finite measurements? Is there any reason a psychologist couldn't use both methods in order to obtain information about human beings that is both rich and precise?[9]

If by *science* we mean only the use of rigorous, empirical and experimental methods, then it must be concluded that the broad field of psychology is not a science. Past efforts have attempted to force psychology into a hard-science mold that could look like physics, but Koch is right when he admits that these efforts have failed. They are likely to fail in the future.

If, in contrast, we think of science as a careful, systematic observation and analysis of data—including data coming from outside the laboratory, from the humanities and from divine revelation—then psychology can be considered a science.

Regrettably, many psychological thinkers have reached conclusions based on biased views of the data, distorted perceptions and loose, sloppy thinking. Such irresponsible data gathering and illogical thinking are seen in all fields of study, but when they appear in psychology, our critics are given reason to charge that psychology is a pseudoscience, not far removed from the magic of witch doctors.

Instead of defending themselves against such charges, psychologists and psychology students can make sure that their own work is of such good quality that critics have no reason to complain.

Is an Emphasis on the Self Really Harmful?

27

Almost ten years ago, I received a book in the mail, an autographed gift from an psychologist in New York. I had never heard of Paul Vitz; but I was fascinated with his thoughtful and well-written little volume.[1]

The book's thesis was simple: Modern psychology has become a cult that worships the self. Beginning with a brief critique of Erich Fromm, Carl Rogers, Abraham Maslow and Rollo May, Vitz described the self-help movement and argued that selfism is bad science, bad philosophy and bad theology.

Overemphasis on the self, suggested the author, has permeated politics, education, marriage, the family, sexual relationships, counseling, book publishing, the women's movement, career building and even the church. Looking ahead, Vitz predicted that people would eventually get bored with the cult of self and seek, instead, to find a different life philosophy.

Has this happened?

Not if we believe some of the more recent observers of psychology. Psychologists[2] and nonpsychologists[3] alike have continued to raise questions and sound the alarm about "self-idolatry."[4] Some have added criticisms of the self-help movement, self-esteem and the whole self-actualization/human potential movement.

Are these critics overreacting? Is the building of self-esteem, the search for self-fulfillment or the actualizing of self-potential really as dangerous as some claim?

Overemphasis on the self can be destructive. Despite the enthusiastic claims of self-theorists, an overemphasis on the self can be harmful and ultimately self-destructive. Self-acceptance, self-esteem, self-gratification, self-fulfillment, self-assertion, self-confidence—these have become widely accepted values in contemporary Western society. Spurred by the writings of modern psychologists and other self theorists, a whole generation has learned to live for its own self-satisfaction. In place of sensitivity and concern for others, responsibility for actions or a willingness to give, many have instead become self-centered, self-pleasing, self-trusting and selfish.

Psychologist Nathaniel Branden has expressed this generation's philosophy concisely: "I cannot think of a single psychological problem—from anxiety and depression, to fear of intimacy or of success, to alcohol or drug abuse, to spouse battering or child molestation, to suicide and crimes of violence—that is not traceable to the problem of a poor self-concept. . . . Positive self-esteem is a cardinal requirement of a fulfilling life."[5]

Such a philosophy appears to motivate egotistical entertainment figures and theological superstars. Politicians scramble to build their own power bases and self-serving careers. Husbands and wives abandon each other because they no longer feel self-fulfilled or willing to make the self-sacrifices needed to build relationships. Students and career-builders ruthlessly compete with one another to boost their grade-point averages and career potential.

It would be a mistake to assume that this self-serving mentality is accepted by everyone. The world is filled with many caring, giving people. We must not conclude that our whole society has been converted to a selfist religion.

Beginning in the Garden of Eden, however, and continuing throughout history, the basis of idolatry has been self-worship: the tendency for humans to put themselves, rather than God, at the center of importance and control. Selfism is at the basis of pride; and pride leads to self-destruction (Prov 16:18).

Underemphasis on the self can be deceiving. The critics of selfism have raised some valid observations, but they often paint a picture that isn't completely accurate. Nathaniel Branden's defense of self theory, for example, does not sound egotistical or self-absorbing:

Currently being attacked as "a religion of self-worship," the movement's exponents are charged with being self-centered, self-indulgent, infantile. And . . . critics imply that a concern with self-realization entails indifference to human relationships and the problems of the world. . . .

Admittedly, there is a lot about the movement that is foolish, irresponsible, even obnoxious—some people's notion of self-assertiveness, for instance. . . . But individualism, self-esteem, autonomy and interest in personal growth are not narcissism—the latter being a condition of unhealthy and excessive self-absorption arising from a deep-rooted sense of inner deficiency and deprivation. . . .

I do not know of a single reputable leader in the human potential movement who teaches that self-actualization is to be pursued without involvement in and commitment to personal relationships. There is overwhelming evidence, including scientific research findings, that the higher the level of an individual's self-esteem, the more likely that he or she will treat others with respect, kindness and generosity.[6]

This is a perspective that critics of selfism rarely report. Aware of the real dangers of pride and overemphasis on self, some have refused to see anything positive in the self-fulfillment literature. Others have tried to ignore the self, to pretend that self isn't important and to overlook our basic human desires for self-fulfillment and a positive self-image.

The world may have distorted viewpoints about the value of self, and there may be too many "foolish, irresponsible, even obnoxious" people in the self-esteem movement, but that does not mean we should try to pretend that the self doesn't exist or that self-fulfillment isn't important.

Jesus gave his followers a clear statement about the self. "If anyone would come after me, he must deny himself and take up his cross daily and follow me" (Lk 9:23). Self-denial involves putting aside selfish desires, self-sufficiency and narrow personal interests. Then we can follow Christ, even if this involves suffering or death.

From this it does not follow that we should talk ourselves into thinking that everything about the self is bad or that the self must be condemned to nonexistence. Too much attention to the self is harmful, but so is too little. Ignoring or squelching the self can create problems and lead to unrealistic, deceptive thinking.

The Bible gives a realistic view of the self. The Bible does not condemn human potential. God's Word acknowledges, instead, that human beings have been created in the divine image, as finite replicas of God. We have dignity, value and purpose. This is not because some humanistic psychology decides that people are valuable, but because the God of the universe created us and declared that his creation was good.

But God's creation fell into sin. Not content to be godlike, humans wanted instead to be sovereign, all-powerful gods. We developed an inflated view of self, a self-deceiving, proud tendency to believe we each can control and manage our own selves, lives and destinies. This thinking is common today.

The Christian, in contrast, believes that humans are sinful and innately self-serving. We do not manage our lives by pretending that self-fulfillment will come as a result of human effort or ingenuity. Instead, we confess our sins, believe that God will forgive and yield ourselves to his control.

He does not demand that we then stamp out all ideas about the self and become passive, lackluster nonentities. On the contrary, he molds us into new creatures with reason for positive self-esteem because we are children of the King. He gives us spiritual gifts, abilities and responsibilities that we can use to serve Christ, help others, and find genuine fulfillment in life. His Holy Spirit helps us develop self-control and creates in us a desire to be serving, caring, giving, encouraging people.

It is not what Branden suggests, a humanly manufactured self-esteem that leads us to treat others with respect, kindness and generosity.[7] Instead, the Holy Spirit works to change people internally, to give us a new self-confidence based on our relationship with Christ and to create in us a sincere desire to reach out and help build the self-concepts of others.

That is true human potential. It does not confuse humanity with deity, and neither does it assume we can completely develop potential and reach "self-actualization" by ourselves. Instead, it asserts that the Supreme God of the universe enables us, through Christ, to find real self-fulfillment. This kind of self-emphasis is not harmful. It gives us hope for positive psychological change in this world and for perfection in the next.[8]

Why Would a Good Christian Ever Attempt Suicide?

28

_H_APPINESS IS A CHOICE!

That was the message of a popular book about depression written several years ago by two Christian psychiatrists. After labeling depression "America's number one health problem," the authors suggested that most human depression results from "our own irresponsible behavior—our own irresponsible handling of our anger and guilt." Some people are irresponsible because they choose to be, the book stated; others are irresponsible because they lack knowledge. In either case, people should face responsibility and learn how to handle their emotions better.[1]

There are times, perhaps more than we care to admit, when all of us get depressed and stay "down." For a while, we wallow in sadness and fail to make the effort, take the responsibility or get the help that would enable us to pull up from the despair. Once we determine to escape this nonbiological depression, we often can find happiness, especially when other people are willing to offer encouragement and help. At such times, happiness is a choice.

But it is neither fair nor realistic to conclude that we can always choose to be happy. Deeply depressed people are rarely if ever able to find relief and "avoid ever being depressed again" simply by reading and applying the message of a Christian self-help book.[2] This is especially true if the depresson has a clear physical cause. When fatigue, chemical imbalances, brain disorders, disease, genetic predispositions or other physical influences lead to depression, there is little that will power or possibility thinking can do to lift the feelings of despair. Without physical change, happiness is *not* a choice.

Sometimes depression comes because we have lost a loved one, separated from a meaningful relationship, or been hurt by the actions of another person. Grief and sadness are natural responses to losses such as these. Even Jesus wept at the tomb of Lazarus (Jn 11:35) and was "sorrowful and troubled" as he prayed in Gethsemane (Mt 26:37). In times of loss and sadness, surely it is harmful and unrealistic to deny our feelings and pretend we can choose to be happy in the midst of such pain. These are times when happiness is *not* a choice.

In those situations, people often make choices about suicide. Would a good Christian ever attempt to take his or her life, especially during a time of great unhappiness or depression?

Like depression, suicide could have a multitude of causes. One writer has suggested that people threaten or attempt suicide to—

☐ get out of what appears to be an intolerable situation
☐ punish survivors and make them feel guilty
☐ gain attention
☐ manipulate others
☐ join a deceased loved one
☐ avoid punishment
☐ punish oneself
☐ avoid becoming a burden to others
☐ avoid the effects of a dread disease

☐ seek martyrdom and

☐ (on rare occasions) act on the basis of an irrational, impulsive whim[3]

You will notice that people who take their lives for reasons such as these are not always depressed. Often there is a feeling of ambivalence—a swinging back and forth between a desire to die and a will to live—before the final decision is made.

When one decides to attempt suicide, is that sin?

Only seven people in the Bible are mentioned as having killed themselves, and all but one are clearly out of God's will.[4] I agree with those who state that suicide is never God's will except when laying down one's life to save others.[5] The Scriptures command us not to kill. Since suicide is the killing of oneself, surely this is sin, just as murder is sin.

From this it does not follow that suicide is the unpardonable sin. Even good Christians fall into sin at times. It may be anger, greed, lust, gluttony or a violent sin. But God offers forgiveness even when the sin is great—as he did with Peter and David. As Christians we believe that "the blood of Jesus . . . purifies us from all sin" (1 Jn 1:7), even if we should die before we can confess every sin to God. Presumably this includes the sin of suicide.[6]

Would a believer in God's will ever choose suicide? Moses, Elijah, Job, David and Jeremiah were all depressed at some time in their lives, but none attempted suicide. Some wanted their lives to end, but there is no evidence that these spiritual giants contemplated self-destruction. They knew that taking a human life is sin, and they chose not to do it.

Not all believers follow their example. With some frequency, counselors see committed Christians and faithful churchgoers whose lives are so filled with despair that they contemplate suicide as the best alternative. These people may know that suicide is wrong, but in the midst of their distress and despondency they irrationally grasp at suicide as perhaps the only way to deal with their problems.

When we are overwhelmed with turmoil, crippled with pain and disease, or burdened with a deep sense of hopelessness, it is difficult to think rationally or to act responsibly. At such times, suicide may seem wise and even good. This doesn't make suicide right, but sometimes even good Christians lapse into sinful behavior and act in self-destructive ways.

I have a friend who went through a severe depression and seriously considered suicide. "I know now that it would have been wrong to kill myself," the friend told me recently. "At the time, however, it seemed like the best alternative." My friend was a good Christian who attended church regularly during those difficult months and managed somehow to pray and read the Scriptures daily. Still, he had no desire to live, and he really believed his family would be better off if he were dead and no longer causing them such concern.

Why is he alive and functioning well today? Undoubtedly the prayers of his friends and family were answered. A counselor's guidance helped keep things in perspective when he tended to think irrationally. His family's love and support encouraged and sustained him when he felt like giving up hope. The care he received from fellow believers helped him bear the burden of depression until he eventually was able to come through his trials. The quiet and powerful sustenance of the Holy Spirit surely brought comfort and protection during a time when he wasn't always alert spiritually.

Had my friend taken his life in spite of all this support, his family and church members would have grieved and felt guilty. Probably the counselor would have been shaken, and if my friend had been young, some of his classmates might have wondered if the fatal choice of suicide should be theirs as well.[7] And my friend would be gone because of his own sinful decision and action.

It is estimated that two million teen-agers will attempt suicide within the next twelve months. Six thousand will succeed. Among adults, suicide is the tenth leading cause of death. Among college students it is the second most common cause. On the day that you read these words over one hundred Americans will kill themselves. Perhaps ten times that many will make a suicide attempt, and an unknown number of others will think about it. It isn't surprising that some call suicide a problem of epidemic proportions.

Among the victims of this suicidal wave will be at least a few committed believers. Good Christians can't always choose to be happy. They do attempt suicide and sometimes, sadly, they succeed.

Is Anything Wrong with Parapsychology and ESP?

*D*OES ESP REALLY EXIST?

Is it possible to read minds?

Can psychic readers predict the future?

Is it possible to use mind power to bend spoons or float objects in space?

Are UFOs real—or do they only exist in people's imaginations?

These are fascinating questions that curious people wonder about but that most psychologists (including Christians) tend to ignore. Probably many students are disappointed when they get no answers to these questions in their psychology courses.

Parapsychology is the study of "psychic phenomena" such as extrasensory perception (knowledge that does not appear to come through the sense organs), precognition (knowledge of events before they occur), telepathy (the ability to read another person's mind) or psychokinesis (the ability of the mind to influence objects).[1] The word *parapsychology* is popularly applied to all kinds of extraordinary events including sightings of ghosts, the Loch Ness monster and unidentified flying objects (UFOs); experiencing poltergeists ("noisy spirits" who are thought to move furniture, break dishes or propel objects through the air), levitation (floating in the air) or mental control over disease; out-of-body experiences (OBEs), hypnosis, palmistry and tarot. Those who claim that parapsychology is a science may be interested in all these phenomena, but as scientists they are inclined to limit their interests to research that tries to demonstrate, understand and explain unusual "paranormal" happenings and abilities.[2]

Do psychic phenomena exist? Many people would answer yes. Often we hear of people whose dreams seem to have predicted some future event, whose premonitions have come to pass or whose extrasensory awareness of some distant happening has later been confirmed. To test the extent of belief in psychic phenomena, psychologists once arranged for magic demonstrations to be given in several university classrooms. Students were told that the performer "does *not* really have psychic abilities, and what you'll be seeing are really only tricks." When they were interviewed later, however, 58% of the students called the performance psychic; only 33% considered it mere magical deception.[3]

Despite the widespread desire to believe in psychic phenomena, it is difficult to support these beliefs with clear data. Spontaneous occurrences, like the premonition of a coming catastrophe, are difficult to document or prove. Attempts to collect reports of psychic experiences began over a century ago, but it is impossible to determine whether or not these subjective reports are valid. Laboratory experiments designed to study psychic phenomena have yielded inconclusive results in spite of hundreds of research projects.[4]

Parapsychology is a controversial field, and there is even disagreement about the validity of research results. Few psychologists are as honest as McGill University's Donald Hebb, who admitted his prejudice against parapsychology and flatly declared: "I do not accept ESP for a moment, because it does not make sense."[5] Some think that the results of parapsychological research "would be regarded as completely convincing if they were in a more conventional field,"[6] but most psychologists probably would agree that parapsychology "is best described as being belief in search of data rather than data in search of explanation."[7]

Can psychic events be studied psychologically? Science must be able to observe facts carefully and accurately, find cause-effect relationships and explain events in accordance with naturalistic laws. Parapsychological research has trouble complying with these requirements. In spite of creative and ingenious research methods, it is difficult to observe psychic events with precision, hard to find cause-effect relationships and often impossible to explain the findings naturalistically.

Before we reject parapsychology for these weaknesses, we should note that many religious experiences, including those Christians consider valid, are also beyond the study capabilities of science. Hebb is to be admired for his honest admission of prejudice, but isn't it narrow and unrealistic to assume that all things in heaven and earth can be studied with precision by the scientific method?

Scientific parapsychological experiments frequently are criticized for poor research design, imprecise collection of data, statistical errors, biased reporting, deliberate fraud or flawed results because of the unconscious transmission of information during experiments. Researchers have attempted to control these influences, but some parapsychologists argue that skeptics will never be convinced no matter how precise the research design or impressive the evidence. Even so, "parapsychology's defenders and critics agree: there has never been a reproducible psychic experiment, nor any individual who can consistently evidence psychic ability."[8]

Can psychic events be explained? Several years ago, popular press reports described the presumed powers of psychic surgeons who claimed to do surgery painlessly and successfully with their bare hands. Thousands of Westerners traveled to the Philippines where they submitted to the "treatment" of healers who later were shown to be frauds and sleight-of-hand artists.[9]

Trickery is only one explanation for presumed psychic events. *Selective perception* means people's tendency to see what they want to see, regardless of what really happens. The human mind has a remarkable ability to let preconceived notions bias the way in which information is interpreted and remembered.[10] A fortuneteller may be wrong most of the time, but one or two accurate predictions may be seen by believers in fortunetelling as proof of precognition. Faulty memory may cause a person to believe that he or she dreamed about some event before it happened. Since there is no way to disprove this claim, belief in psychic prediction through dreams is accepted. The many dreams that don't "predict" future events are quickly forgotten.

All these explanations leave the Christian with one big question. Is it possible that some psychic events have no psychological explanation but are, instead, evidence of supernatural influences? At times, doesn't the Holy Spirit supernaturally alert believers to pray for another person who is in a special time of need? Paul felt divine leading in his missionary work, and sometimes he sensed that travel was being hindered by supernatural forces. God can and does influence human beings supernaturally.

But so can Satan. The devil and his false prophets are able to perform signs and miracles that are convincing even to Christians (Mt 24:24). Some of the psychic events that interest parapsychologists could be Satanic gimmicks that distract people from the gospel and lead instead to fascination with deceptive signs and wonders. The strong biblical warnings against sorcery—seeking answers or influencing events by psychic means—should alert us to the dangers of involvement with phenomena that might be occult (Lev 20:6; Deut 18:10-12; Acts 19:18-19).[11]

As we have seen, the branch of study known as *apologetics* attempts to challenge and answer those critics who attempt to undercut the Christian faith.[12] In view of the current popular interest in psychic events and parapsychology, shouldn't apologists be answering those who raise questions about ESP and related phenomena? A few Christian psychologists are writing in this area, but most ignore the issue.[13]

Parapsychology is a controversial but serious attempt to study unusual psychic events. Christians should not ignore or completely dismiss this field of study; believers dare not leave the study of imagined and real supernatural events to those who cannot understand phenomena that must be spiritually discerned (1 Cor 2:14).

Is There Power in Positive Thinking?

Y OU CAN IF YOU THINK YOU CAN!

When the going gets tough, the tough get going!

It is always too soon to quit!

Plugging away will win the day!

Change your thinking and you'll change the world!

Never take no for an answer!

Never think of failing—You don't have to!

The slogans seem endless. They come from motivation experts, supersalesmen, dynamic preachers, high-powered psychologists and self-help authors. The words differ but the message is similar: all things are possible to one with a positive mental attitude.

There is no doubt that negative thinking can make life miserable.[1] People who fall into the trap of bitterness, faultfinding, constant criticism and cynicism often go through life expecting everything to get worse. Often that is exactly what happens. When we expect the worst, we do nothing to prevent our expectations from coming true. Negative thinking thus helps bring about the things we most fear.

In contrast, a positive mental attitude (known sometimes as PMA) creates hope, reduces pessimism, leads to a happy disposition, stimulates people to cope with the pressures of life and motivates them to action. Little wonder that PMA is a popular message. It promises success, gives easy-to-follow formulas, and often guarantees victory over failure and frustration. The possibility speakers are themselves models of being on top of life. They make little mention of defeat, pain, sin, unhappiness or the need for hard work, long years of education and investment capital. Instead, they tell us to visualize success, never say no, motivate ourselves with positive self-talk and "keep on keeping on"—going against all odds until our goals are reached. This is popular psychology in its most powerful and most visible form.

Perhaps it is not surprising that many psychologists and theologians have criticized this viewpoint. The mental rehearsal of positive slogans can motivate and encourage people, but mental images do not create reality. Fantasy can be fun, but in contrast to the lyrics of an old song, wishing will *not* always "make it so." Despite the exuberant claims of positive thinkers,[2] some problems do not fade in response to enthusiastic thinking and an upbeat mental attitude.

Sometimes positive thinking can lead us to ignore problems and deny reality. By looking at things optimistically, it is possible to overlook real danger and miss seeing severe problems. This happened often in the Old Testament. The prophets would call people to repentance, but the masses would prefer to see things positively and ignore the realities of political corruption or moral decline in their society.

Similar attitudes exist today. Positive thinking can be a smoke screen that hides reality, enables people to deny their weaknesses and provides an excuse to do nothing about problems that may, in time, be destructive.

Psychiatrist M. Scott Peck once wrote that laziness is the biggest impediment to spiritual and personal growth.[3] Patients come to counselors wanting things to be different, but they have little real desire to work for change. The lazy person doesn't want to make the effort to accomplish things. It seems easier and less risky to do as little as possible. If we are all lazy, as Peck suggests, we all prefer to avoid any actions that might bring failure, discomfort or inconvenience.

There can be no doubt that the positive-thinking advocates have done much to counter this attitude. They have encouraged many people, motivated others to action and challenged the poor-little-me-I-can't-do-anything mentality. But positive thinkers tend to forget that some people do not have the abilities, training or opportunities to attain their unrealistic dreams or reach their lofty goals. Like all enthusiasts, the possibility thinkers emphasize success stories but fail to tell about people who had a positive mindset and failed.

Sometimes positive thinking can undermine basic Christianity. The very positive ideas that reduce pessimism, help people cope with pressure, and stimulate action can also overlook and even undercut some core biblical teachings.

The Bible teaches that God loves us, values us, cares for us and gives us hope. The God who created the world and us is still in control, holding all things together by his power. Individuals who confess their sins and acknowledge the lordship of Christ become his children, assured of eternal life with him in a place without sorrow or defeat. Because they believe this, Christians have every reason to shun pessimism and think positively—about themselves, about the world and about the future.

From this it does not follow that life on earth will always be happy and beautiful. The Bible realistically warns of life's dangers, freely deals with unpopular subjects like sin, and alerts us to the results of immorality. It calls readers to repentance, shows that people are powerless apart from God (despite what they might think), and realistically states that believers may be persecuted or thrown into prison. Some of history's greatest saints did not make it to the top in their societies, even though they served God diligently and had a positive mindset.

Positive thinkers say little about obedience, discipleship, discipline, self-denial or the cost of commitment. And they rarely mention the will of God for individual lives.

The Bible never implies that God wants us to have a positive mental attitude that ignores our dependence on him and sends us off on self-centered schemes to get pleasure, acclaim and success. God wants obedience, sensitivity to his leading, and a recognition of sin and the realities of life. Christ himself taught that the way to be great is to be a servant (Mt 20:25-27), even though this may not lead to a life of ease and happiness. The Christian's responsibility is to yield to God's control and direction, knowing that he will give a realistic and hopeful perspective on life.

The slogans of the positive thinkers motivate people. They stimulate optimism and encourage people to persist in their efforts even when they feel like failures. Positive thinkers challenge depressed and negative people—many of whom are miserable, hypercritical, pessimistic Christians. A strong jolt of powerful positive thinking could benefit the many believers who talk and sing about joy but instead are bogged down by their ungodly sour mental attitudes.

Balanced thinking is more realistic. This is optimistic thinking that acknowledges God's sovereignty and is sensitive to his will. It is thinking that knows all things are possible with Christ—even those impossible with humans alone (Mt 19:26). It is thinking that is yielded to God's control and direction, knowing he will give a realistic perspective on this life and the next.

Without this biblical balance, positive thinking may still be powerful—but it may not be healthy or right.

Is Psychology Its Own Worst Enemy?

Postscript

Pogo was a possum, the hero of a comic strip drawn many years ago by a creative man named Walt Kelly.

It was a strangely humorous comic strip about sophisticated animals sitting under trees, riding on rafts and discussing social issues in a lazy swamp. When I was in college, Pogo was especially popular among students who appreciated its philosophical wisdom and frequent political satire.

Perhaps you've read one of Pogo's most famous statements. It still is quoted, long after the death of the comic strip and its insightful creator: "We have found the enemy—and it's us!"

In the preceding pages we have looked at some questions people frequently ask about psychology. We have mentioned some of psychology's critics and tried to deal with their criticisms in an honest, straightforward way. But the preceding questions have made me wonder, at times, if psychology might be creating many of its own problems.

Are psychologists, including Christian psychologists, at least partially responsible for the hot debates that surround their profession? Is it possible that we who study and work in the field of psychology have found the enemy—and it's us?

Too often, it seems, psychology creates unnecessary controversy and condones unbiblical compromise.

Unnecessary controversy. It is easy to condemn our critics for their methods and arguments, but psychologists sometimes use tactics that are similar. Critics give almost no research evidence to support claims that their methods are superior. Psychologists try to be more research oriented, but many make their own sweeping statements without adequate support.

Critics tend to imply guilt by association. One writer, for example, talks about psychoanalysis, Jim Jones and Charles Manson all in the same eighteen-word sentence.[1] Linking analysts with bizarre and deviant psychopaths is both inaccurate and inflammatory. It may be, however, that we psychologists stimulate the controversy by treating critics as the critics treat us—by unfairly and inaccurately linking them with undesirable groups and narrow-minded people.

Critics have been accused of lifting material out of context, quoting selectively and distorting what was originally written.[2] Are we psychologists guilty of similar practices? To misquote people and cause them to say what they never intended is unfair and unethical, whether we are psychologists or critics.

Critics sometimes appear to be angry people. Anger isn't always bad. Jesus was angry when he encountered hypocrisy, spiritual deadness and self-serving attitudes. Usually, however, he treated people with kindness. He knew that "a gentle answer turns away wrath, but a harsh word stirs up anger" (Prov 15:1). Although he condemned injustice, he never gave evidence of being an innately hostile person. This can't be said of all psychologists. Some respond to criticism with the same hostility, character assassination and cynicism that many critics (including Christian critics) use against psychology. Doesn't this stir up further controversy?

Critics sometimes lump diverse people, psychological methods and theories all together under some label that is then attacked. But all advocates of self-esteem are not trying to establish a new cult that worships the self. All counselors who use self-talk are not humanists. All psychologists do not think alike. The followers of Rogers and Freud often are no more similar than members of radically different Christian denominations. Clinical psychologists, experimentalists, transpersonal psychologists, secular humanists and Christian therapists may all belong to the same profession, but they are not all the same. It is as wrong to condemn a whole profession because of some of its members as to criticize the whole Christian religion because of its fanatic and cultic fringes.

Psychologists in turn must not respond as if all critics are ill informed, illogical and self-serving. Some critics are thoughtful, sensitive, knowledgeable, caring people whose criticisms are valid and well worth heeding.

Unbiblical compromise. Gordon MacDonald has observed that most criticisms contain at least a kernel of truth. This surely applies to the criticisms of contemporary psychology. There *is* a tendency for some psychologists to criticize or explain away religious experience, naively and uncritically embrace mystical occult practices, proclaim the effectiveness of their methods without giving empirical evidence or other convincing proof, overemphasize the self, undermine traditional family and sexual values, produce simplistic self-help books, preach a humanistic religion and make pronouncements in the name of science that are little more than personal opinion. Of course there is much that is wrong about psychology—but there is also much that is sensitive, helpful, valid and good. The best psychologists carefully sift the conclusions and evidence, reject that which is invalid and make use of the rest.

How do we determine what is invalid? It helps to look at research evidence, logical deductions and pragmatic reports showing whether or not ideas are workable. But for the Christian, there is another criterion against which psychology must be evaluated: the teachings of Scripture. The non-Christian is unlikely to understand or accept this principle, but the believer assumes that the Word of God is a true standard against which all other knowledge must be tested.

If we could peek into the classrooms, laboratories or counseling sessions of many Christian psychologists, I wonder if we would always see behavior and attitudes consistent with biblical teaching.

Would we see counselors who gently but boldly raise the issue of sin when they talk to counselees?

Would we see counselors who pray for and sometimes with their counselees?

Would we see helpers who respect professional ethics and individual freedom of choice, but who also are careful never to condone values and practices that the Bible calls immoral?

Would we see counselors quoting Scripture and sharing biblical principles?

Might we also find counselors who have indeed sold their evangelical birthright for a mess of psychological pottage?

Might we see counselors who name the name of Christ on Sunday but whose psychological work in no way differs from that of their secular colleagues?

Might we see Christian therapists who encourage outbursts of vehement anger, unhealthy fantasies or dangerous occultlike practices assumed to bring healing and relief?

Might we find psychologists who are unaware of the dangerous trends in their profession, hypercritical of colleagues who take a clearer Christian stand, smugly self-satisfied about their "liberation" from more traditional biblical values or discreetly silent about the beliefs their churches proclaim on Sunday?

Psychologists who claim to be Christians sometimes hide their Christianity well. Is it any wonder that they are criticized for condoning unbiblical compromise?

Shortly after I started work on this manuscript, I received a letter from a friend encouraging me to abandon the project. "A book like that might hurt your career," he wrote. "It will harm sales of your other books and create the impression that you are a reactionary."

Since the beginning of this century, critics have been attacking psychology with increasing vehemence. Within the past two decades, negative Christian critiques have grown in frequency and intensity. Isn't it time somebody started to give balanced answers to the criticisms—even if this might hurt careers or create wrong impressions?

Christians within psychology (and without) have the challenge of living and serving in two worlds—the secular world where we work and the Christian world where we belong. We must avoid the extreme of completely rejecting secular influences that could be used to serve the Lord and help other people. But we must also avoid the extreme of enthusiastically incorporating trends that are deceptively beautiful but in reality very harmful.

How we handle psychology and how we relate it to the Christian faith are issues of far greater importance than the subjects of those college debates we mentioned at the beginning of this book.

Even Pogo would agree.

Notes

Preface

[1]Albert Ellis, "The Case Against Religion," *Mesa Journal* 138 (September 1970). Reprints available from the Institute for Rational Living, 45 East 65th Street, New York, NY 10021.

[2]Paul C. Vitz, *Psychology as Religion: The Cult of Self-Worship* (Grand Rapids, Mich.: Eerdmans, 1977), p. 9.

[3]Martin L. Gross, *The Psychological Society* (New York: Simon and Schuster, Touchstone, 1978).

[4]Quoted in Bernie Zilbergeld, *The Shrinking of America: Myths of Psychological Change* (Boston: Little, Brown, 1983), p. 114. See also Garth Wood, *The Myth of Neurosis: Overcoming the Illness Excuse* (New York: Harper & Row, 1986).

[5]Jay E. Adams, *Competent to Counsel* (Grand Rapids, Mich.: Baker, 1970), p. 1.

[6]Ibid., p. 7.

[7]Martin and Deidre Bobgan, *The Psychological Way/ The Spiritual Way: Are Christianity and Psychotherapy Compatible?* (Minneapolis: Bethany, 1979), p. 49.

[8]William Kirk Kilpatrick, *The Emperor's New Clothes: The Naked Truth about Psychology* (Westchester, Ill.: Crossway, 1985), p. 4.

[9]These ideas are expressed in William Kirk Kilpatrick, *Psychological Seduction: The Failure of Modern Psychology* (Nashville: Nelson, 1983).

[10]Dave Hunt, *Beyond Seduction* (Eugene, Oreg.: Harvest House, 1987), p. 130. A similar conclusion is expressed in a recent book that calls "Christian psychology" a "confusion of contradictory theories and techniques." See Martin and Deidre Bobgan, *Psychoheresy: The Psychological Seduction of Christianity* (Santa Barbara, Calif.: Eastgate, 1987), p. 5.

[11]Jimmy Swaggart, "Christian Psychology?" *The Evangelist*, November 1986, p. 7.

Chapter 1: Can You Trust Psychology?

[1]Bernie Zilbergeld, *The Shrinking of America: Myths of Psychological Change* (Boston: Little, Brown, 1983), p. 271.

[2]Bernie Zilbergeld, "Myths of Counseling," *Leadership* 5, no. 1 (Winter 1984):87-94.

[3]Ibid., p. 93.

[4]Dave Hunt, *Beyond Seduction* (Eugene, Oreg.: Harvest House, 1987), p. 145.

[5]Our textbook in my seminary class defined theology as "the science of God and of the relations between God and the universe." A. H. Strong, *Systematic Theology* (Old Tappan, N.J.: Revell, 1907), p. 1.

Chapter 2: Why Should a Christian Get Counseling If God Can Meet All Our Needs?

[1]Jimmy Swaggart, "The Behavioral Sciences: Psychology, Sociology, and Psychiatry," *The*

Evangelist, August 1984, pp. 7-8.

²For an excellent discussion of Jesus' style of relating see David E. Carlson, "Relationship Counseling," in Gary R. Collins, *Helping People Grow* (Ventura, Calif.: Regal, 1980), pp. 31-54. (This book is now out of print.)

Chapter 3: Why Go to Psychologists If They Never Help Anyone?

¹Richard and Deanne Mincer, *The Talk Show Book* (New York: Facts on File Publications, 1982), p. xi.

²Bernie Zilbergeld, *The Shrinking of America: Myths of Psychological Change* (Boston: Little, Brown, 1983). See especially chapters 2—6.

³Ibid., pp. 39, 86.

⁴Hans J. Eysenck, "The Effects of Psychotherapy: An Evaluation," *Journal of Consulting Psychology* 16 (1952):322.

⁵Martin and Deidre Bobgan, *The Psychological Way/The Spiritual Way* (Minneapolis: Bethany, 1979), p. 24.

⁶Ibid.

⁷Dave Hunt and T. A. McMahon, *The Seduction of Christianity* (Eugene, Oreg.: Harvest House, 1985), p. 205.

⁸Roger Mills, "Psychology Goes Insane, Botches Role as Science," *The National Educator,* July 1980, p. 14.

⁹A. E. Bergin, "The Effects of Psychotherapy: Negative Results Revisited," *Journal of Counseling Psychology* 10 (1963):244-50.

¹⁰Allen E. Bergin and Michael J. Lambert, "The Evaluation of Therapeutic Outcomes," in Sol L. Garfield and Allen E. Bergin, eds., *Handbook of Psychotherapy and Behavior Change: An Empirical Analysis,* 2d ed. (New York: Wiley, 1978), p. 140.

¹¹Ibid., p. 148.

¹²Interested readers can find a massive survey of this data in Garfield and Bergin (see note 10).

¹³Gary R. Vanden Bos, "Psychotherapy Research: A Special Issue," *American Psychologist* 41 (February 1986):111.

¹⁴Bergin and Lambert, p. 152.

¹⁵Ibid., pp. 159-60.

¹⁶Ibid., pp. 162, 170. See also William B. Stiles, David A. Shapiro, and Robert Elliot, "Are All Psychotherapists Equivalent?" *American Psychologist* 41 (1986):165-80.

¹⁷Ibid., p. 170.

¹⁸Zilbergeld, p. 271.

¹⁹L. E. Beutler, "Values, Beliefs, Religion and the Persuasive Influence of Psychotherapy," *Psychotherapy: Theory, Research and Practice* 16 (1979):432-40.

Chapter 4: Should a Christian Ever Go to a Non-Christian Counselor?

¹E. L. Worthington, Jr., and G. G. Scott, "Goal Selection for Counseling with Potentially Religious Clients by Professional and Student Counselors in Explicitly Christian or Secular Settings," *Journal of Psychology and Theology* 11 (1983):318-29.

[2]L. E. Beutler, "Values, Beliefs, Religion and the Persuasive Influence of Psychotherapy," *Psychotherapy: Theory, Research and Practice* 16 (1979):432-40; L. E. Beutler, S. Pollack, and A. M. Jobe, "Acceptance: Values and Therapeutic Change," *Journal of Consulting and Clinical Psychology* 46:198-99; A. E. Bergin, "Psychotherapy and Religious Values," *Journal of Consulting and Clinical Psychology* 48 (1980):95-105.

[3]L. E. Beutler, A. M. Jobe, and D. Elkins, "Outcomes in Group Psychotherapy: Using Persuasion Theory to Increase Treatment Efficiency," *Journal of Consulting and Clinical Psychology* 42:547-53. The quotation, taken from page 552, is reported in Everett L. Worthington, Jr., "Religious Counseling: A Review of Published Empirical Research" *Journal of Counseling and Development* 64 (March 1986):421-31.

[4]Worthington, "Religious Counseling," p. 427.

[5]D. G. Cross and J. A. Khan, "The Values of Three Practitioner Groups: Religious and Moral Aspects," *Counseling and Values* 28 (1983):13-19; W. E. Henry, J. H. Sims, and S. L. Spray, *The Fifth Profession: Becoming a Psychotherapist* (San Francisco: Jossey-Bass, 1971).

Chapter 5: Should Christians Take Therapeutic Drugs?

[1]This is the opinion of E. Fuller Torrey, *The Mind Game* (New York: Emerson-Hall, 1972). Dr. Torrey notes that mood-altering drugs are not limited to Western cultures. They are used all over the world, even in primitive cultures.

[2]Garth Wood, *The Myth of Neurosis: Overcoming the Illness Excuse* (New York: Harper & Row, 1986).

[3]Ibid., p. 106.

[4]M. Scott Peck, *The Road Less Traveled* (New York: Simon & Schuster, Touchstone, 1978), p. 15.

[5]See Wood, pp. 99, 104-6; and Peck, pp. 15-32.

[6]R. J. Salinger, "Psychopharmacology," in David G. Benner, ed., *Baker Encyclopedia of Psychology* (Grand Rapids, Mich.: Baker, 1985), 944-49.

[7]David V. Sheehan, *The Anxiety Disease* (New York: Charles Scribner's Sons, 1983).

[8]Wood, p. 108.

[9]These results are new and, at this writing, not yet available in professional journals. See "Talk Is as Good as a Pill," *Time*, 26 May 1986, p. 60; and "Quick-Fix Therapy," *Newsweek*, 26 May 1986, pp. 74-76.

Chapter 6: Why Is Professional Counseling So Expensive?

[1]Garth Wood, *The Myth of Neurosis* (New York: Harper & Row, 1986), p. 266. Since Dr. Wood is highly critical of the "psychotherapy industry," his figures may be unrealistically high.

[2]"Quick-Fix Therapy," *Newsweek*, 26 May 1986, pp. 74-76.

[3]William Herron and Suzanne Sitkowski, "Effects of Fees on Psychotherapy: What Is the Evidence?" *Professional Psychology: Research and Practice* 17 (August 1986):347-51.

[4]This is the term used by Bernie Zilbergeld, *The Srinking of America: Myths of Psychological Change* (Boston: Little, Brown, 1979), pp. 87-113.

[5]See, for example, James Hilt, "Professionals Must Adjust Their Fees," *Christianity Today*, 6 February 1987, p. 30. Some have noted that Hilt works for a Christian organization that

pays his salary—so he has no overhead expenses and little need to charge a fee.
[6]Zilbergeld makes this point clearly. He gives several reasons why people who have caring friends still prefer to consult professionals. Some of these counselees have greater faith in professionals, are reluctant to share intimate details with friends or feel more comfortable talking with a stranger. See Zilbergeld, p. 273.

Chapter 7: Are Lay Counselors as Effective as Professionals?

[1]J. A. Durlak, "Comparative Effectiveness of Paraprofessional and Professional Helpers," *Psychological Bulletin* 86 (1979):80-92.

[2]H. H. Strupp and S. W. Hadley, "Specific vs. Nonspecific Factors in Psychotherapy," *Archives of General Psychiatry* 36 (1979):1125-36.

[3]Garth Wood, *The Myth of Neurosis: Overcoming the Illness Excuse* (New York: Harper & Row, 1986), p. 286.

[4]Ibid., p. 30.

[5]Robert R. Carkhuff, "Differential Functioning of Lay and Professional Helpers," *Journal of Counseling Psychology* 15 (1968):117-26.

Chapter 8: What Is Unique about Christian Counseling?

[1]As a rule I try to avoid repeating in one book what I have said previously in another. In the following paragraphs, however, I will restate, sometimes word for word, a previous summary of the uniquenesses of Christian counseling. The topic is discussed in more detail in Gary R. Collins, *Helping People Grow* (Ventura, Calif.: Regal, 1980), pp. 322-27.

[2]For further discussion, see Gary R. Collins, *The Rebuilding of Psychology* (Wheaton, Ill.: Tyndale, 1977).

[3]Before publication, a perceptive evaluator of this manuscript noted that in writing about Christian counselors, "Collins clearly has a certain rather rare breed of professional in mind, that being Christian psychologists who are competent professionally and draw effectively on the secular discipline while retaining their evangelical commitment to Christianity and applying that commitment to their professional activities. . . . He is defining an ideal, not a sizable bunch of real people." This, I suspect, is true. It supports the sad observation with which I began this chapter: many who call themselves Christian aren't much different from counselors who are blatantly secular.

Chapter 9: Is There a Spiritual Way to Counsel That Is Better Than the Psychological Way?

[1]Martin and Deidre Bobgan, *The Psychological Way/The Spiritual Way* (Minneapolis: Bethany, 1979).

[2]The quoted phrase comes from Bobgan and Bobgan, p. 184. Each of the other adjectives in this sentence is used at some place in their book to describe psychotherapy. I suspect the authors would have no quarrel with my one-sentence summary, which I believe is a fair and valid statement of their position.

[3]Ibid., p. 193.

[4]Martin and Deidre Bobgan, *How to Counsel from Scripture* (Chicago: Moody, 1985). The quotation is from page 7.

[5]Ibid., p. xv.

[6]Harvard psychologist Gordon Allport, for example, once wrote a secular book about religion in which he argued that love as described in 1 John 4 is "incomparably the greatest psychotherapeutic agent—something that professional psychiatry cannot of itself create, focus, nor release." Gordon Allport, *The Individual and His Religion* (New York: Macmillan, 1950), p. 90.

[7]Erwin W. Lutzer hints at this view. "I suspect that if we'd take the time to analyze the text, we would find that such psychological insights are already in the Scriptures." See Erwin W. Lutzer, "Toward a Philosophy of Counseling," *Moody Monthly*, February 1983, p. 81.

[8]Ibid.

[9]This difference between the cure of the mind and the cure of souls is a major point of Bogban and Bobgan, *How to Counsel from Scripture.*

Chapter 10: Does Christian Counseling Always Work?

[1]Jimmy Swaggart, "The Behavioral Sciences: Psychology, Sociology, and Psychiatry," *The Evangelist*, August 1984, p. 9.

[2]See, for example, books by Lawrence J. Crabb, Jr., *Effective Biblical Counseling* (Grand Rapids, Mich.: Zondervan, 1977); Paul Welter, *How to Help a Friend* (Wheaton, Ill.: Tyndale, 1978); Everett L. Worthington, Jr., *When Someone Asks for Help: A Practical Guide for Counseling* (Downers Grove, Ill.: InterVarsity, 1982). I summarized some Christian approaches to counseling in Gary R. Collins, ed., *Helping People Grow* (Ventura, Calif.: Regal, 1980).

[3]Martin and Deidre Bobgan, *The Psychological Way/The Spiritual Way* (Minneapolis: Bethany, 1979), p. 18.

[4]Martin and Deidre Bobgan, *Psychoheresy: The Psychological Seduction of Christianity* (Santa Barbara, Calif.: Eastgate, 1987), p. 94.

[5]Everett L. Worthington, Jr., "Religious Counseling: A Review of Published Empirical Research," *Journal of Counseling and Development* 64 (March 1986):421-31. Dr. Worthington is an evangelical who has published books with InterVarsity Press and Word.

[6]Ibid., p. 429.

Chapter 11: Why Are There So Many Different Approaches to Christian Counseling?

[1]Hans H. Strupp, "Psychotherapy Research and Practice: An Overview," in Sol L. Garfield and Allen E. Bergin, eds., *Handbook of Psychotherapy and Behavior Change*, 2d ed. (New York: Wiley, 1978), p. 3.

[2]F. H. Garrison, *Introduction to the History of Medicine* (Philadelphia: Saunders, 1921).

[3]1 Corinthians 12; Romans 12:3-8; Ephesians 4:11-13.

[4]Henry A. Virkler, *Hermeneutics: Principles and Processes of Biblical Interpretation* (Grand Rapids, Mich.: Baker, 1981), p. 16.

[5]There are several helpful books on hermeneutics. Virkler, cited above, is a psychologist with theological training. A classic and very practical book is Bernard Ramm, *Protestant Biblical Interpretation*, 3d ed. (Grand Rapids, Mich.: Baker, 1970).

[6]William Glasser, *Reality Therapy* (New York: Harper & Row, 1965).

[7]Jay E. Adams, *Competent to Counsel* (Grand Rapids, Mich.: Baker, 1970). See, for example,

p. 70.

[8]Charles R. Solomon, *Counseling with the Mind of Christ* (Old Tappan, N. J.: Revell, 1977).

[9]For an overview of Christian counseling approaches, with emphasis on evangelical approaches, see Gary R. Collins, ed., *Helping People Grow: Practical Approaches to Christian Counseling* (Ventura, Calif.: Regal, 1980).

[10]William B. Stiles, David A. Shapiro, and Robert Elliott, "Are All Psychotherapies Equivalent?" *American Psychologist* 41 (February 1986):165-80.

[11]Everett L. Worthington, Jr., "Religious Counseling: A Review of Published Empirical Research," *Journal of Counseling and Development* 64 (March 1986):429.

Chapter 12: Why Would a Christian Counselor Use Secular Counseling Methods?

[1]Everett L. Worthington, Jr., "Religious Counseling: A Review of Published Empirical Research," *Journal of Counseling and Development* 64 (March 1986):421-31.

[2]Martin and Deidre Bobgan, *How to Counsel from Scripture* (Chicago: Moody, 1985), p. 42.

[3]This question is discussed in more detail in chapter 24.

[4]Bobgan and Bobgan, *How to Counsel from Scripture*. The book jacket describes this book as an "invaluable guide to biblical counseling."

[5]Ibid., p. 13.

[6]Ibid., p. 61.

[7]Ibid., p. 190.

[8]Bobgan and Bobgan list all these as biblical techniques.

Chapter 13: Can Christian Counselors Help Non-Christians?

[1]L. E. Beutler, S. Pollack, and A. M. Jobe, "Acceptance: Values and Therapeutic Change," *Journal of Consulting and Clinical Psychology* 46 (1978):198-99.

[2]Ibid. See also Everett L. Worthington, Jr., "Religious Counseling: A Review of Published Empirical Research," *Journal of Counseling and Development* 64 (March 1986):421-31.

[3]Jay E. Adams, *Competent to Counsel* (Grand Rapids, Mich.: Baker, 1970), p. 67.

Chapter 14: Should a Christian Bother to Get Counselor Training?

[1]E. Fuller Torrey, "Hollywood's Pique at Psychiatry," *Psychology Today*, July 1981, pp. 74-79.

[2]"Quick-Fix Therapy," *Newsweek*, 26 May 1986, pp. 74-76.

[3]J. A. Durlak, "Comparative Effectiveness of Paraprofessional and Professional Helpers," *Psychological Bulletin* 86 (1979):1125-36.

[4]These ideas are elaborated more fully in Gary R. Collins, *How to be a People Helper* (Santa Ana, Calif.: Vision House, 1976), pp. 60-62.

[5]Paul Morris, *Love Therapy* (Wheaton, Ill.: Tyndale, 1974), pp. 16-17.

Chapter 15: Is Mental Health the Same as Christian Maturity?

[1]A number of books and articles have attempted to deal with the issue of mental health and maturity. See, for example, Vernon C. Grounds, "Holiness and Healthymindedness," *Journal of Psychology and Theology* 2 (1974):3-11; J. Roland Fleck and John D. Carter, eds., *Psychology and Christianity: Integrative Readings* (Nashville: Abingdon, 1981); and H. Newton Malony, ed.,

Wholeness and Holiness (Grand Rapids, Mich.: Baker, 1983).

[2]O. H. Mowrer, "What Is Normal Behavior?" in E. A. Berg and L. A. Pennington, eds., *Introduction to Clinical Psychology*, 2d ed. (New York: Ronald, 1954), pp. 58-88.

[3]Gary R. Collins, *Fractured Personalities* (Carol Stream, Ill.: Creation House, 1972), pp. 10-12. There is a problem with this analysis. If mental health involves being at peace with ourselves, at peace with society and at peace with God, it may be that mental health is not completely possible.

[4]This list is adapted from John C. Carter, "Maturity: Psychological and Biblical," *Journal of Psychology and Theology* 2 (1974).

[5]Gordon.W. Allport, *The Individual and His Religion* (New York: Macmillan, 1950).

[6]Gordon W. Allport, *Becoming* (New Haven: Yale, 1955).

Chapter 16: Jesus and Paul Never Used Psychology—So Why Should We?

[1]Jay E. Adams, *More Than Redemption: A Theology of Christian Counseling* (Grand Rapids, Mich.: Baker, 1979), p. 16.

[2]Martin and Deidre Bobgan, *How to Counsel from Scripture* (Chicago: Moody, 1985), p. 8. One critic has challenged them by asking, "How do we know that the church was successful before psychology?" We know that the church ministered. It is only an assumption that they ministered successfully.

[3]Erwin W. Lutzer, "Toward a Philosophy of Counseling," *Moody Monthly*, February 1983, p. 81.

[4]Dave Hunt and T. A. McMahon, *The Seduction of Christianity* (Eugene, Oreg.: Harvest House, 1985), p. 209.

[5]Martin and Deidre Bobgan, *The Psychological Way/The Spiritual Way* (Minneapolis: Bethany, 1978), p. 11.

[6]This is a major concern expressed by Hunt and McMahon, p. 209.

Chapter 17: What Good Is Psychology If the Bible Tells Us All We Need to Know?

[1]Jay E. Adams, *The Christian Counselor's Manual* (Nutley, N.J.: Presbyterian and Reformed, 1973), p. 23.

[2]Martin and Deidre Bobgan, *The Psychological Way/The Spiritual Way* (Minneapolis: Bethany, 1979), p.11.

[3]Erwin W. Lutzer, "Toward a Philosophy of Counseling," *Moody Monthly*, February 1983, p. 81.

[4]I believe this statement without reservation. I also believe that the Bible is without error (inerrant) in its original writings, that it contains all the information we need to know about salvation, and that it is the final authority on how to live and what to believe.

Chapter 18: Is Psychology a New Religion That Competes with Christianity?

[1]Bernie Zilbergeld, *The Shrinking of America: Myths of Psychological Change* (Boston: Little, Brown, 1983), p. 32. In the June 1986 issue of *Science*, it was estimated that there are more than 160,000 professional therapists in the United States alone.

[2]Quoted in Zilbergeld, p. 87.

[3]Jerome D. Frank, "An Overview of Psychotherapy," *Overview of the Psychotherapies*, Gene Usdin, ed. (New York: Brunner/Mazel, 1975), p. 7.

[4]Paul C. Vitz, *Psychology as Religion: The Cult of Self-Worship* (Grand Rapids, Mich.: Eerdmans, 1977).

[5]The term is suggested by Martin L. Gross, *The Psychological Society* (New York: Simon and Schuster, Touchstone, 1978), pp. 55-92.

[6]Ibid., p. 57.

[7]Dave Hunt, *Beyond Seduction* (Eugene, Oreg.,: Harvest House, 1987), p. 136.

[8]This is Vitz's main conclusion in *Psychology as Religion*.

Chapter 19: Does Psychology Dabble in the Demonic?

[1]C. S. Lewis, *The Screwtape Letters* (Glasgow: Collins, Fontana Books, 1942), p. 9.

[2]Ralph Metzner, *Maps of Consciousness* (New York: Macmillan, 1971).

[3]Jacob Needleman, *A Sense of the Cosmos* (Garden City, N.Y.: Doubleday, 1975), p. 109.

[4]William Kirk Kilpatrick, *The Emperor's New Clothes* (Westchester, Ill.: Crossway, 1985), pp. 129-84.

[5]Martin and Deidre Bobgan, *The Psychological Way/ The Spiritual Way* (Minneapolis: Bethany, 1978), pp. 199-200.

[6]In his book *Beyond Seduction* (Eugene, Oreg.,: Harvest House, 1987) Dave Hunt notes that there are numerous legitimate uses of imagination and visualization. I agree with Hunt's warning that visualization is potentially harmful and in danger of opening individuals to occultism when it implies that the visualized person or object is somehow brought up into reality, when we visualize dreams of success and conclude that these are evidences of God's will for our lives or when one assumes that visualization "exercises or triggers a mysterious force that causes to occur in the real world what has been visualized in the imaginary one." See Hunt, pp. 198-201.

[7]For a professional Christian counselor's perspective on these issues see H. Norman Wright, *Self-Talk, Imagery, and Prayer in Counseling* (Waco, Tex.: Word, 1986).

[8]David A. Seamands, *Healing of Memories* (Wheaton, Ill.: Victor, 1985).

Chapter 20: Does Psychology Explain Away Biblical Miracles?

[1]For a concise and clear critique, see Norman L. Geisler, *Miracles and Modern Thought* (Grand Rapids, Mich.: Zondervan, 1982), p. 82.

[2]C. S. Lewis, *Miracles: A Preliminary Study* (London: Collins, Fontana, 1947); see p. 138.

[3]For a discussion of the Lourdes shrine see Alan Neame, *The Happening at Lourdes: The Sociology of the Grotto* (New York: Simon & Schuster, 1967). See also Claude A. Frazier, ed., *Faith Healing: Finger of God? or Scientific Curiosity?* (Nashville: Nelson, 1973).

[4]See, for example, William A. Nolen, *Healing: A Doctor in Search of a Miracle* (New York: Random House, 1974). For a less objective but more sympathetic treatment, see Allen Spraggett, *Kathryn Kuhlmann: The Woman Who Believes in Miracles* (New York: Signet, New American Library, 1970).

[5]After investigating the psychic surgeons, Nolen wrote: "I've flown almost eight thousand miles trying to find something miraculous to write a book about, and all I've found so far

are a lot of sleight-of-hand artists. And not very good ones at that" (ibid., p. 211).

[6]I have discussed this in my book on the mind: Gary R. Collins, *Your Magnificent Mind* (Grand Rapids, Mich.: Baker, 1985).

[7]C. S. Lewis, quoted in *Your Magnificent Mind*, p. 168.

[8]Ibid., p. 169.

[9]John Weldon and Zola Levitt, *Psychic Healing: An Exposé of an Occult Phenomenon* (Chicago: Moody, 1982); and Johanna Michaelsen, *The Beautiful Side of Evil* (Eugene, Oreg.: Harvest House, 1982).

[10]S. Freud, *The Future of an Illusion* (New York: Doubleday Anchor, 1927).

[11]For an in-depth consideration of healings, see Morton T. Kelsey, *Healing and Christianity* (New York: Harper & Row, 1973). A balanced Christian treatment of the topic is presented by Roy Lawrence, *Christian Healing Rediscovered* (Downers Grove, Ill.: InterVarsity, 1980).

Chapter 21: Are Psychological Problems All Caused by Sin?

[1]Jay E. Adams, *Competent to Counsel* (Grand Rapids, Mich.: Baker, 1970), pp. 61, 18.

[2]It also is probable that some differences reflect professional jealousy and competition. Psychiatrists, for example, have long resisted the intrusion of psychologists and others into the fee-charging counseling professions. In turn, psychologists have resisted the psychiatrists' claim that medically trained people alone are competent to "treat mental illness," charge fees and be paid by insurance companies.

[3]Martin and Deidre Bobgan, *The Psychological Way/The Spiritual Way* (Minneapolis: Bethany House, 1979), pp. 41-42.

[4]Much of it has been summarized in an earlier book. See Gary R. Collins, *Your Magnificent Mind* (Grand Rapids, Mich.: Baker, 1985).

[5]The next few paragraphs are drawn from Crabb's analysis. See Lawrence J. Crabb, Jr., *Effective Biblical Counseling* (Grand Rapids, Mich.: Zondervan, 1977), pp. 40-47.

[6]Ibid., p. 43.

Chapter 22: Can Christians Study Secular Psychology without Undermining Their Faith?

[1]Sigmund Freud, *The Future of an Illusion* (New York: Norton, 1961 [orig. ed. 1927]).

[2]Erich Fromm, *Psychoanalysis and Religion* (New Haven: Yale, 1950), p. 49.

[3]See, for example, Will Herberg, *Protestant, Catholic, Jew* (Garden City, N.Y.: Doubleday, 1955); and Martin E. Marty, *The Shape of American Religion* (New York: Harper, 1959). This American religion and its relationship to Fromm's ideas is discussed in J. Stanley Glen, *Erich Fromm: A Protestant Critique* (Philadelphia: Westminster, 1966).

[4]Glen, p. 24.

[5]These are Marty's observations in *The Shape of American Religion*.

[6]Paul C. Vitz, *Psychology as Religion: The Cult of Self-Worship* (Grand Rapids, Mich.: Eerdmans, 1977), p. 108.

[7]Allen E. Bergin, "Psychotherapy and Religious Values," *Journal of Consulting and Clinical Psychology* 48 (1980):95-105.

[8]William Kirk Kilpatrick, *The Emperor's New Clothes* (Westchester, Ill.: Crossway, 1985), pp. 178-79.

Chapter 23: Why Is Psychology Taught in Seminaries and Bible Colleges?

[1]P. E. Adolph, "Healing, Health," in Merrill C. Tenney, ed., *The Zondervan Pictorial Encyclopedia of the Bible,* vol. 3 (Grand Rapids, Mich.: Zondervan, 1975), p. 54.

[2]See, for example, Charles R. Smith, "What Part Hath Psychology in Theology?" *Journal of Psychology and Theology* 3 (Fall 1975):272-76.

[3]William Dyrness, *Christian Apologetics in a World Community* (Downers Grove, Ill.: InterVarsity, 1983).

Chapter 24: Can Secular Psychology and Christianity Be Integrated?

[1]Jay E. Adams, Response to "Myths of Counseling," *Leadership* 5 (Winter 1984):93.

[2]William Kirk Kilpatrick, *Psychological Seduction* (Nashville: Thomas Nelson, 1983), p. 23.

[3]Ibid.

[4]William Kirk Kilpatrick, *The Emperor's New Clothes* (Westchester, Ill.: Crossway, 1985), p. 20.

[5]Jimmy Swaggart, "The Behavioral Sciences: Psychology, Sociology, and Psychiatry" *The Evangelist,* August 1984, p. 8. See also Jimmy Swaggart, "Christian Psychology?" *The Evangelist,* November 1986, pp. 4-9.

[6]Craig W. Ellison, preface to David G. Myers, *The Human Puzzle: Psychological Research and Christian Belief* (New York: Harper & Row, 1978), p. xii.

[7]For a helpful discussion of the integration issue see John C. Carter and Bruce Narramore, *The Integration of Psychology and Theology* (Grand Rapids, Mich.: Zondervan, 1979).

[8]Kirk E. Farnsworth, *Whole-Hearted Integration* (Grand Rapids, Mich.: Baker, 1985), p. 11.

[9]In a recent book, psychologist Kirk Farnsworth addresses this issue. Evangelical psychologists talk much about integration, but Farnsworth has written one of the first books to suggest how it should be done.

[10]This quotation is taken from my Finch lectures at Fuller Theological Seminary. Gary R. Collins, *Psychology and Theology: Prospects for Integration* (Nashville: Abingdon, 1981), p. 83.

[11]Martin and Deidre Bobgan, *The Psychological Way/The Spiritual Way* (Minneapolis: Bethany, 1979), pp. 168-72.

[12]A. White, *A History of the Warfare of Science with Theology in Christendom* (New York: Appleton, 1898), p. 137.

Chapter 25: Is Mental Illness a Myth?

[1]Thomas S. Szasz, *The Myth of Mental Illness* (New York: Harper & Row, 1961).

[2]Psychiatrist E. Fuller Torrey, for example, is another well-known critic. He writes that "the medical model of human behavior, when carried to its logical conclusions, is both nonsensical and nonfunctional. It doesn't answer the questions which are asked of it, it doesn't provide good service, and it leads to a stream of absurdities. . . ." E. Fuller Torrey, *The Death of Psychiatry* (Radnor, Pa.: Chilton, 1974), p. 24.

[3]Ibid., p. 262.

[4]Garth Wood, *The Myth of Neurosis: Overcoming the Illness Excuse* (New York: Harper & Row, 1986).

[5]E. Fuller Torrey, *The Mind Game* (New York: Emerson Hall, 1972).

[6]Thomas Szasz, *The Myth of Psychotherapy* (Garden City, N. Y.: Doubleday Anchor, 1978).
[7]Each of these myths is presented in books that currently are in print.

Chapter 26: Is Psychology Really a Science?

[1]As every scientist knows, however, this is ideal. Many so-called scientific facts are not accurate, and experiments are often poorly planned, biased and not reliable. The good scientist, of course, strives to avoid these weaknesses.

[2]Sigmund Koch, ed., *Psychology: A Study of a Science* (New York: McGraw-Hill, 1959-63).

[3]Sigmund Koch, "Psychology Cannot Be a Coherent Science," *Psychology Today,* September 1969, p. 66. Italics his.

[4]This is the term used by Martin and Deidre Bobgan, *The Psychological Way/The Spiritual Way* (Minneapolis: Bethany, 1979), p. 43.

[5]This view is proposed by E. Fuller Torrey, *The Mind Game: Witchdoctors and Psychiatrists* (New York: Emerson Hall, 1972).

[6]*The Living Webster Encyclopedia Dictionary of the English Language* (Chicago: The English Language Institute of America, 1977).

[7]Ibid.

[8]Michael Wertheimer, *Fundamental Issues in Psychology* (New York: Holt, Rinehart and Winston, 1972).

[9]I made an appeal for this "expanded empiricism" in Gary R. Collins, *The Rebuilding of Psychology* (Wheaton, Ill.: Tyndale, 1977).

Chapter 27: Is an Emphasis on the Self Really Harmful?

[1]Paul C. Vitz, *Psychology as Religion: The Cult of Self-Worship* (Grand Rapids, Mich.: Eerdmans, 1977).

[2]For example, David G. Myers, *The Inflated Self* (New York: Seabury, 1981); William Kirk Kilpatrick, *Psychological Seduction* (Nashville: Nelson, 1983), and William Kirk Kilpatrick, *The Emperor's New Clothes* (Westchester, Ill.: Crossway, 1985).

[3]For example, Dave Hunt and T. A. McMahon, *The Seduction of Christianity* (Eugene, Oreg.: Harvest House, 1985); Dave Hunt, *Beyond Seduction* (Eugene, Oreg.: Harvest House, 1987); and Jay E. Adams, *The Biblical View of Self-Esteem, Self-Love, Self-Image* (Eugene, Oreg.: Harvest House, 1986).

[4]This term is that of Hunt and McMahon, but Vitz also calls self-worship a form of idolatry.

[5]Nathaniel Branden, "Restraints May Allow Fulfillment," *APA Monitor,* October 1984, p. 5.

[6]Ibid.

[7]See the quotation earlier in this chapter.

[8]Douglas R. Groothuis, *Unmasking the New Age* (Downers Grove, Ill.: InterVarsity, 1986), p. 91.

Chapter 28: Why Would a Good Christian Ever Attempt Suicide?

[1]Frank B. Minirth and Paul D. Meier, *Happiness Is a Choice* (Grand Rapids, Mich.: Baker, 1978). The quotation is from page 44.

[2]This is the suggestion of Tim LaHaye, *How to Win Over Depression* (Grand Rapids, Mich.:

Zondervan, 1974), p. 12.

[3]Bill Blackburn, *What You Should Know about Suicide* (Waco, Tex.: Word, 1982).

[4]Abimelech (Judg 9:54), Samson (Judg 16:30), Saul (1 Sam 31:4), Saul's armor-bearer (1 Sam 31:5), Ahithophel (2 Sam 17:23), Zimri (1 Kings 16:18) and Judas (Mt 27:5). Samson's case may be an exception. He was involved in a war against the Philistines and could be said to be bringing God's judgment against them. The point has been much debated by Christians over the years and many still disagree after careful study.

[5]Minirth and Meier, p. 34. Dying to save others is not an act of suicide but of sacrificial love. As Jesus said, "Greater love has no one than this, that he lay down his life for his friends" (Jn 15:13).

[6]I realize that some Christians may disagree with me at this point.

[7]This tendency of teen-age suicides to run in groups is discussed by John Q. Baucom, *Fatal Choice: The Teenage Suicide Crisis* (Chicago: Moody, 1986).

Chapter 29: Is Anything Wrong with Parapsychology and ESP?

[1]Technically, extrasensory perception (ESP) is an umbrella term that includes precognition, telepathy and clairvoyance (knowledge of hidden objects and distant events).

[2]A good overview of parapsychological research can be found in Benjamin B. Wolman, ed., *Handbook of Parapsychology* (New York: Van Nostrand Reinhold, 1977). For more critical perspectives, see James E. Alcock, *Parapsychology: Science or Magic?* (New York: Pergamon, 1981), and Leonard Zusne and Warren H. Jones, *Anomalistic Psychology: A Study of Extraordinary Phenomena of Behavior and Experience* (Hillsdale, N.J.: Lawrence Erlbaum Associates, 1982).

[3]V. A. Benassi, B. Singer, and C. B. Reynolds, "Occult Belief: Seeing Is Believing," *Journal for the Scientific Study of Religion* 19 (1980):337-49.

[4]Much of this research was conducted under the direction of Duke University's J. B. Rhine, who spent most of his professional life doing parapsychology research. Some of this research is summarized in a brief but excellent introduction to parapsychology, K. R. Rao, "Parapsychology," in Raymond J. Corsini, ed., *Encyclopedia of Psychology* 2 (1984):478-82.

[5]Reported in Rao, pp. 478-82.

[6]Rao, "Parapsychology."

[7]Alcock, p. ix.

[8]David G. Myers, "ESP and the Paranormal: Supernatural or Super-fraud?" *Christianity Today* 27 (15 July 1983):14-17.

[9]For a discussion of psychic surgery, see William A. Nolen, *Healing: A Doctor in Search of a Miracle* (New York: Random House, 1974).

[10]Myers, "ESP and the Paranormal."

[11]For a discussion of parapsychology from a Christian perspective, see the article by R. D. Kahoe in David G. Benner, ed., *Baker Encyclopedia of Psychology* (Grand Rapids, Mich.: Baker, 1985), pp. 793-97.

[12]This is the theme of one book on apologetics: Frederic R. Howe, *Challenge and Response: A Handbook of Christian Apologetics* (Grand Rapids, Mich.: Zondervan, 1982).

[13]One such book is by Danny Korem and Paul Meier, *The Fakers: Exploding the Myths of the*

Supernatural (Old Tappan, N.J.: Revell, 1980). For a fascinating Christian analysis of occult phenomena, see John Weldon and Zola Levitt, *Psychic Healing: An Exposé of an Occult Phenomenon* (Chicago: Moody, 1982).

Chapter 30: Is There Power in Positive Thinking?

[1]Some of the material in this chapter is adapted from two of my previous books: Gary R. Collins, *Calm Down* (Ventura, Calif.: Vision House, 1981), chap. 10; and Gary R. Collins, *Your Magnificent Mind* (Grand Rapids, Mich.: Baker, 1985), chap. 4.

[2]For a historical overview of positive thinkers, see Donald Meyer, *The Positive Thinkers: Religion as Pop Psychology from Mary Baker Eddy to Oral Roberts* (New York: Pantheon, 1965).

[3]M. Scott Peck, *The Road Less Traveled* (New York: Simon & Schuster, 1978), pp. 271-77.

Postscript: Is Psychology Its Own Worst Enemy?

[1]"Moreover, psychoanalysis is based on theories no less bizarre than anything Jim Jones or Charles Manson subscribed to." Dave Hunt, *The Cult Explosion* (Eugene, Oreg.: Harvest House, 1980), p. 69.

[2]Robert L. Wise, "Welcome to the Inquisition," *Christianity Today* 30 (16 May 1986):18.

Index